CHIN
FACE &
HAND
READING

CHINESE POPULAR CLASSICS

This new and innovative Chinese Popular Classics series will take you to the heart of the Chinese world. One quarter of the world's population is Chinese, yet the great and ancient culture of China is barely known in the West. This is especially true of the popular beliefs which have shaped folk religion and culture in China for over 2000 years. These beliefs offer insights and understanding of relevance for the wider world and are increasingly being recognised as significant religious and spiritual teachings. What was in the past often dismissed by the scornful West as superstition or peasant lore, is now seen to reflect centuries of wisdom.

The team behind the series comes from the International Consultancy on Religion, Education and Culture (ICOREC) who for over twelve years have led the way in translating Chinese religious texts. It is headed by Martin Palmer, whose translations of Chinese texts have established him as one of the foremost interpreters of Chinese religion in the UK today. The team brings together Taoist priests, monks, organisations such as the China Taoist Association, feng shui masters, scholars of classical Chinese, poets and researchers, both in the UK and China. With their assistance it is possible to explore the mythological and philosophical, practical and mystical worlds of popular Chinese culture.

To understand China you need to understand her soul. Through this series, such a journey of exploration can begin.

CHINESE
POPULAR CLASSICS

CHINESE FACE & HAND READING

TRANSLATED BY MAN-HO KWOK

EDITED BY

JOANNE O'BRIEN

SERIES EDITOR

MARTIN PALMER

PIATKUS

Acknowledgements

Our gratitude to our friends and colleagues at ICOREC, Elizabeth Breuilly and Josephine Edwards. We would also like to express our thanks to our editor, Anne Lawrance.

The cover embroidery is a detail from a Chinese silk panel from the early Ming Dynasty – probably from the fifteenth century. It is woven with a design of small boys holding prunus flower stems. Each boy is wearing a bib and baggy trousers, the hair cut short except for three small bunches. The design of many small boys was frequently used in China and symbolised the wish for male offspring. It was often used for wedding hangings and wedding gifts. The tapestry is reproduced courtesy of Spink and Son Ltd, London.

First published in 1995 by
Judy Piatkus (Publishers) Ltd
5 Windmill Street, London W1P 1HF

A catalogue record for this book is available
from the British Library

ISBN 0-7499-1467-X

Designed by Chris Warner
Illustrations by One-Eleven Line Art
Chinese woodcuts © Circa Photo Library

Set in 11/13pt Sabon by
Action Typesetting, Gloucester

Printed and bound in Great Britain by
Biddles Ltd, Guildford & King's Lynn

CONTENTS

INTRODUCTION:
FACING THE FUTURE

OUR LANGUAGE is full of phrases summing up a belief that personality is in the face. 'He has shifty eyes'; 'She has a cruel face'; 'You can see the kindness in his eyes', are just a few of the many examples. And to the Chinese of old, all this was not just old wives' tales or chance. Over thousands of years the Chinese have developed one of the most comprehensive systems for reading fortunes in people's faces that exists anywhere.

In this book we have distilled some of the basic insights, teachings and ways of practising this ancient and honoured art, known as physiognomy. For millennia, Chinese emperors, rulers, sages and teachers have used this method to understand a person's nature and future. Now you can do the same.

How often have you judged someone by the look in their eyes or on their face? Are you attracted to people by the way they move or mistrust them because they have a cold stare or a hard mouth? Without knowing it we make assumptions about someone's character by their physical appearance or because they remind us of a certain animal or bird.

In the art of Chinese hand, face and body reading these associations are not coincidental. Each feature, line and shape has a meaning which affects our character, relationships and destiny. This system of reading your body reflects many traditional Chinese beliefs. Great importance is placed upon long life, prosperity, respect, and happy, fruitful, family relations. These are the essential features of any Chinese fortune-telling, be it by horoscope or divination sticks, *I Ching* prediction or this, the art of physiognomy. For at heart all Chinese wish to know what the future will bring them – as indeed do most people.

Exactly how and where many of the readings associated with the body's features come from is unknown. The earliest records we have date back to over two hundred years before Christ to a time when China underwent a terrible upheaval.

In the late 1970s a remarkable set of figures was discovered near Xian in China. Thousands upon thousands of life-size terracotta warriors were unearthed which date back to c. 220 BC. These soldiers had been buried to defend in death the most brutal and powerful ruler China had ever experienced. His name was Chin Shi Huang Ti and he was the first to unite the whole of China, albeit under the heel of a massive army of over one and a half million soldiers. His armies destroyed the old culture of China and he tried to finish this off by burning all books so that no one would know that life could ever be other than the way it was under his rule.

He failed, but the shock to Chinese life with its model of a stable world of just rulers was immense. Out of this confusion and the realisation that the rulers of this world were not to be trusted, came a desire to be in touch with a deeper knowledge, with a more certain form of understanding. At about this time, much of what are now the fortune-telling and divinational practices of China first came into existence. And amongst these was physiognomy. We know this because it was vigorously attacked by the philosopher Hsun Tzu in the third century BC.

In the first century BC we find the great historian of China, Ssu Ma Chien, commenting upon a practitioner of these arts, Kuei Ku Tzu – the Devil Valley Master. So we can safely say that physiognomy has been practised for well over 2000 years in China.

Because China has always been male-dominated, at least since the time physiognomy first began to be practised, many of these readings were originally given for Chinese men. They were considered to be of greater importance because it was through them that the family name descended, and in a world of ancestor worship it was the male ancestors that counted. But China and the system have both changed and most of the readings in this book are relevant to men and women of all races.

The information given in this book is based on the three most popular and common Chinese physiognomy books, all of which have been written in the last thousand years. The oldest is the *Ma-i* (c. 1000 AD), which is considered the jewel in the crown of Chinese physiognomy and undoubtedly draws upon traditions and masters stretching back to before the time of Christ. It was followed by the *Pa P'u Tzu* (c. 1400 AD). Pa P'u Tzu was a practitioner of the arts who lived during the Ming dynasty (1368–1644) and was renowned for his skills in physiognomy. The most recent of all is the *Golden Scissors* (1700 AD). This book summarises the teachings of the others.

Throughout these books run the triple threads of Taoism, Confucianism and Buddhism. Taoism, the oldest-rooted faith of China, pictures a world where the spiritual world, the superior world, breaks through into the mundane material world, if you have eyes to see it. Through trances, the shamans of old, who were the ancestors of the Taoist priests, could communicate with the spiritual world. Through the Taoist priests and practitioners of physiognomy, this ability has come to add its own distinctive ingredient to the art of physiognomy. Confucianism, teaching respect of elders and a strict code of honour and conduct, also underpins this art. For if we obey the rules of proper behaviour then we will be at peace and at ease with ourselves and this will manifest itself in our appearance. Finally, Buddhism, with its theory of reincarnation, says that who you are now is a direct result of what you did in your last life. Thus reflected in the very way you look is a clue to your previous life. If in this life you improve and become more moral, then this will likewise manifest itself in the appearance you have in the next life.

Today, throughout the Chinese world, you will find these books pored over, studied and used. From the tops of China's sacred mountains to the back streets of Chinatowns around the world, fortunes are told through the eyes of the physiognomist. Now these insights are available to a wider audience.

FATE OR PRE-DESTINATION

The concept of fate or predestination shaping our lives is linked to the Taoist tradition of ancestor worship. Taoism is one of the earliest religious systems with which the art of physiognomy would have come into contact. Venerating the ancestors and fulfilling one's duties through religious ceremonies were important features of this tradition. One's inheritance and destiny were in part determined by the ancestors and it was up to the individual to care for this inheritance. If the individual chose to break away from tradition, from the family and from what would be regarded as correct behaviour, his or her actions could herald disaster. Everyone had a responsibility not just for the people around them but also for their physical environment.

This tradition is based on the belief that there is an underlying order and harmony to all life; this is known as the Tao or the Way. The Tao or order of life is established by Heaven and it is up to each family to follow the path destined for them so that the overall harmony of society can be maintained. Although your fate was ultimately decreed by Heaven, there was nevertheless room for personal action, preferably to benefit society. The core principle behind the idea of fate or 'ming' is summed up in the following quotation:

> 'Certain specific incidents were beyond human power once they had been decreed by Heaven and certain lasting aspects of the personal endowment from Heaven could not be altered ... but generally speaking there was no predetermined blueprint that prevented a man from following the dictates of his evaluating mind; nor did any antecedent plan prevent action in accordance with the moral sense from aiding the establishment of an ordered society.'

The Concept of Man in Early China, Donald J. Munro

In essence, while certain factors in your life are beyond your control, others are open to change. You are able to prevent, intervene in or encourage circumstances which have been decreed by Heaven. This is the important difference between the Chinese concept of fate and the western concept of unalterable fate that sweeps us along and is beyond our control. The Chinese belief is summed up in the following story:

P'eng Cho and the Eight Immortals

P'eng Cho spent his day ploughing the fields with his oxen or harvesting the rice crop. He was only fourteen years old but it was a job he had to do since his father died. His mother relied on her only son to support her.

One morning a fortune-teller stopped by the fields and silently watched P'eng Cho. He called him over and looked carefully into his face:

'I have looked at the five features of your face and have studied your physiognomy. I must warn you that you will die on your twentieth birthday.'

P'eng Cho said nothing in reply and the fortune-teller continued on his journey. That evening he told his mother what the fortune-teller had predicted. She was heartbroken but what could she do? The wise man must have given an accurate prediction.

Five years later the Eight Immortals were walking by P'eng Cho's paddy fields and decided to cut across the narrow, raised paths that divided the watery fields. To prevent the water from the plough splashing them, P'eng Cho pulled his oxen to a halt. He offered them food from his meagre lunch and water from his jar but they refused, thanked him and continued on their way. As they walked by he bowed his head in respect. That evening he told his mother in detail about the eight strangers who had crossed his field. From his description she knew that he had met the Eight Immortals and told him to ask them for help if they ever passed his field again.

Two days later, the day before P'eng Cho's twentieth birthday, the final day of his life, the Eight Immortals passed by. The boy's heart jumped with excitement and he and the oxen knelt down in front of the holy people. The Eight Immortals wanted to know what was troubling him and P'eng Cho revealed the fortune-teller's prediction. P'eng Cho pleaded with the men in front of him.

'I know it is within your power to help me. If I die the fields will go to ruin, my mother will be homeless, the lands of our ancestors will be deserted and no one will be left to venerate them. Please grant me my life.'

The holy men and women were so impressed with the young boy's devotion that they promised him a long life so he could serve his mother well. They each gave P'eng Cho the gift of a hundred years of life, then they disappeared. P'eng Cho dropped his hoe in excitement and as it fell it killed a poisonous snake coiled at his feet. This was the snake that would have killed P'eng Cho just as the fortune-teller had predicted.

CONFUCIUS

It was the path of a responsible Taoist to recognise the opportune moment and to act virtuously for the benefit of all. The teachings of Confucius strongly reinforced reverence for the ancestors and duty towards the family and society. Just as we display inherited physical characteristics from our family, we also display a moral and ethical inheritance which should be maintained and enhanced. Although strict Confucian thinkers rejected the notion of inherited fate, these elements were already established as part of traditional Chinese thought, and so the art of physiognomy found a comfortable home in traditional Chinese religion.

BUDDHISM AND KARMA

The belief in karma, that our past, present and future condition is shaped by the consequences of our actions, is central to Buddhist practice. It is also one of the underlying principles of physiognomy. Your character and circumstances at birth are shaped by actions in previous lives, and the law of karma continues to operate at every stage and every moment of your life. You are never a victim of fate.

The core teachings about rebirth and karma are captured in the story of Fa Hien, the great Buddhist monk who travelled to India to collect Buddhist sutras.

One day Fa Hien was cutting rice with many of his fellow disciples when they were ambushed by hungry thieves who tried to force them to hand over their rice. All the monks fled except for Fa Hien who stood up to the thieves and firmly rebuked them, saying, 'If you must have the grain take what you please. But remember that it was your former neglect of charity which brought you to your present state of destitution, and now you want to rob others again. In the coming years you will have greater poverty and distress. I am sorry for you beforehand.' And with these words he went away and the thieves slunk off, leaving the grain.

One of the ways in which karma is expressed is in the bodily manifestation of your next life. This is most harshly expressed in traditional Chinese belief and in physiognomy by the teaching that physical handicaps reflect harmful actions in a previous life. Even though the art of physiognomy did not arise out of Buddhism, it is likely that physiognomy found a logical and philosophical basis in Buddhism.

FATE AND KARMA

In the art of physiognomy there are certain perimeters which are predestined such as your family and place of birth, but what you make of your life is in your hands. Because there are set readings in the book for features on the face or lines on the hands this does appear to contradict the power you have to change your fate. In Chinese physiognomy, however, the two are compatible.

Since your basic physical features are unlikely to change, you are given a specific reading but this does not mean that you are tied to this reading for life. A compassionate or thoughtful act will override a negative forecast. Not only will the circumstances of your life change but aspects of your physical appearance may also change.

One of the main arguments that was, and still is, targeted against physiognomy readings is that people fulfil the reading which is given to them instead of taking control of their own lives. If an individual is convinced that something is going to happen then they make it happen, subconsciously or otherwise.

Physiognomy is not meant to dictate your life and neither is it an absolute forecast. It is a guide to your personality and way of life but the law of karma will come into operation; what you cause has an inescapable effect for good or bad. This double-sided approach is illustrated in the following story.

The Monk and the Tea Boy

High in the mountains of China there lived a Buddhist monk who was a respected teacher of physiognomy. A boy had been sent by his parents to study with this famous monk. The boy read his books in the morning, helped with the meals and listened to the monk as he gave advice to the many people who visited his cave. Sometimes people paid to have a reading but if they could not afford it the monk would never refuse help.

One morning as the boy was pouring the monk's tea, the monk noticed that the boy's complexion had changed. His eyes were becoming cloudy and his skin sallow. The monk decided to calculate what this could mean and asked the boy to give him the paper upon which his mother had written the year, month, day and time of his birth.

The monk began his calculation and for many hours he repeated his examination of the boy's face and hands, but always came up with the same reading: the boy would die within ten days. The monk did not disclose this information to the boy but told him to pack his belongings quickly and return to his parents. The boy begged the master to tell him what he had done wrong but the monk would not give an explanation. He kept repeating, 'Go home to your parents as quickly as you can.'

One month passed and the tea boy was still alive and healthy at his parents' house. His parents told him to return to his master since he was sure to need the boy's help. The tea boy gathered his belongings in a small sack and set off into the mountains.

The monk was lighting a fire as the tea boy came into view down the hill. He couldn't understand why the boy was still alive. He welcomed him back and once again examined his physiognomy. It still told that same story that the tea boy must die soon. He asked the boy to tell him exactly what had happened since they had last seen each other.

The tea boy had set off on his journey home. On the day he left it had been so hot that he had stopped to rest by a steam. As he lay down he saw thousands of ants clambering over an ant hill at the water's edge. He realised that as soon as the rains arrived the ant hill would be swept downstream and the ants drowned. And so he built a protective wall of mud and stones around the hill and bound his underwear around it as an extra safeguard.

The monk knew then why the boy had been saved. 'You were going to die but your life has been spared since you saved the lives of so many ants.'

THE SIGNS AND SYMBOLS OF CHINESE PHYSIOGNOMY

Many of the terms used in hand, face and body readings are practical expressions of ideas found throughout Chinese religious practice and philosophy. (Indeed, one core concept in Chinese thought is that the body itself is a microcosm of the universe – that all that exists is found reflected in our own bodies.) Of these ideas the three most important are the Five Elements, the Five Sacred Mountains, and the Triad of Heaven, Earth and Humanity.

The Five Elements

In Chinese creation myths, life is produced and maintained through the dynamic interaction of yin and yang. Yin is cool, feminine and watery while yang is dark, male and hot. The forces of yin and yang are continually moving and changing at an individual level and at a cosmic level. An angry mood or a hot fever is a sign of strong yang whereas influenza or a withdrawn, contemplative mood indicates strong yin. Yang is at its peak in the height of summer and in the depth of winter yin is strongest.

The interaction of yin and yang also produces the Five Elements – water, fire, metal, earth and wood. Everything in the universe contains these elements to a greater or lesser extent. They are not divine forces, but the forces of nature. Yet they constantly struggle to overcome each other and must be kept in balance.

The Five Elements are not meant to literally represent the physical phenomena whose names they bear. Instead they have certain characteristics and they can be correlated with everything that exists in the universe. The notion of the Five Elements is an ancient one and is thought to have been given or revealed in the earliest times of Chinese history. They are found as the basic structure in all aspects of classic or ancient Chinese thought and are at work in physiognomy (see page 20).

The elements relate to each other in negative or positive combinations. This is the traditional way of describing their interaction:

WATER produces WOOD but overpowers FIRE
FIRE produces EARTH but overpowers METAL
METAL produces WATER but overpowers WOOD
EARTH produces METAL but overpowers WATER
WOOD produces FIRE but overpowers EARTH

These elements are seen in the shape and nature of each individual in differing proportions, and they too have their positive and negative effects on us. A water-shaped person with a fire nature will have a water-type personality since the fire element will be subservient to the dominant water nature.

The Five Sacred Mountains

The belief in the Five August Rulers and their Sacred Mountains is one of the earliest Chinese beliefs. These rulers and mountains express the cardinal points of the Chinese compass and the cardinal colours. The five cardinal points are south (which is placed at the top, unlike western compasses), north, west, east and centre. These mountains, such as Mount T'ai in the east, have always been centres of pilgrimage and continue to be so to the present day. The mountains and rulers are ascribed to the following cardinal points:

CENTRE   The Yellow Emperor at Central Peak in Honan
SOUTH   The Red Emperor at Southern Peak in Hunan
WEST   The White Emperor at Western Peak in Shensi
NORTH   The Black Emperor at Northern Peak in Chihli
EAST   The Green Emperor at Eastern Peak in Shantung

In traditional Chinese thought the world was dominated by these five mountains – they were seen as the highest points on earth reaching towards Heaven. They were believed to be where Heaven and Earth touched, where the spiritual and the material met each other. They were places of immense power. To this day they are centres of pilgrimage and their power is invoked in Taoist ritual across China. These are both literal mountains and mountains reflected in ourselves. In physiognomy, the plane of the face is dominated by the Five Mountains of the forehead, cheeks, nose and chin.

Heaven, Earth and Humanity

In Chinese religious tradition there is a special and powerful relationship between the forces of Heaven, Earth and Humanity. In an ancient classic text described as the *Li Chi* or *Book of Rites* their relationship is described:

Of all the creatures born of Heaven and nourished by the Earth, there is none greater than man.

Li Chi, in *The Sacred Books of the East*, trans. James Legge

Heaven and Earth are believed to be the father and mother of all that exists and humanity is the fulfilment of that union. The triad of Heaven, Earth and Humanity is finely balanced and reflects the harmony of yin and yang. Humans have the power to maintain or disrupt this balance through their actions. At an individual level this could be through violent or selfish acts or at a communal level through war or environmental destruction.

In this overall scheme, the Emperor of China was the human link between Heaven and Earth, and known as the Son of Heaven. Through his wise rule the state could prosper; through his weakness or indecision the state could be weakened and decay. If natural disasters arose, beyond those which might be normally expected, then it was believed that the Mandate of Heaven by which the Emperor ruled had been withdrawn and rebellion was thus permissible. This attitude still persists to this day and major earthquakes, fires or floods are still interpreted in China, even Communist China, as signs that nature rejects the current ruler/system.

The power of Heaven, Earth and Humanity in Chinese thought is attested in physiognomy by the names given to the three areas of the face. For just as in the popular saying 'man is heaven and earth in miniature', so the face is the fate of the individual in miniature.

UNDERSTANDING MODERN PHYSIOGNOMY

Regardless of its religious aspects and ancient links with traditional Chinese culture, the art of palmistry and physiognomy has not been without its critics down the centuries. Some saw it as a manipulation of religious traditions, some as superstition, and others as a means of beguiling a naive audience, convincing them to part with their money or manipulating their actions.

Since the Communists came to power in 1949 practices such as physiognomy have been severely censored. However, in recent years, as religions find a new measure of freedom, cultural and religious traditions are also gaining popularity. Whereas in places like Hong Kong or Singapore you will find the stalls of physiognomists around all the major temples – often scores of them – in China they are not openly on display, but everyone knows where they are. In places where physiognomists can practise openly, such as Hong Kong and Taiwan, they are especially busy during the big festivals such as Chinese New Year. But they have a steady stream of visitors throughout the year seeking guidance about marriage or business ventures. In mainland China the hidden physiognomists are likewise busiest at festivals. To find them, ask and you will be taken a few steps away from the main street to where the practitioners and all their paraphernalia are discreetly positioned. The abiding belief in physiognomy is likely to outlive the belief in Marxist-Leninist-Mao Tse Tung thought!

It is not clear whether major texts such as the *M'ai* or the *Golden Scissors* are still being published by Buddhist temple presses. In the White Cloud Temple in Beijing, centre of the China Taoist Association, they are all to be found on sale although many seem to come from outside China. Nevertheless, these books are being printed again in China by the many new commercial publishing houses which have sprung up in recent years. Regardless of where and how the texts are being printed, their popularity is considerable amongst those visiting centres like White Cloud Temple.

TAKING YOUR READING

For most of us, it is impossible to visit a practising physiognomist in the Far East or in deepest China. And even if we could get there, language and culture would present so many barriers as to make communication impossible. This is why we have prepared this book. In the chapters to come we lead you into the fascinating world of the art of physiognomy as practised for over two thousand years in China. Through translating the texts and weaving into this the knowledge and understanding of living practitioners of the art, and gearing it towards western readers, we have created a doorway into this strange and powerful world.

What follows is an opportunity to explore the fundamental rules and teachings of Chinese physiognomy. Here is all that you need to know to undertake a good initial reading. You may not be able to go to a physiognomist yourself, but with this book we can bring the spirit and insights of this ancient art to you.

WHERE TO BEGIN

There is no hard and fast rule on how to begin taking your reading. If you want a complete reading you can follow each chapter, working your way from the hands to the body and on to the face. You can combine the readings and assess the points or characteristics which emerge. If two readings contradict each other, it doesn't mean your reading is incorrect – it is, in effect, giving you an indication of the possibilities ahead or the variations in your character. You don't even have to begin with Chapter 1: if you are more interested in facial features you can start with any one of the later chapters. Or you can just open the book and dip in to reveal the meaning of a particular feature.

Always remember as you go through the book that, in the end, you control your fate. Your face or hands or body express what is within. It is up to you whether this remains as it is or changes. There is nothing fatalistic about Chinese belief although at first glance it may appear so. What we are can be read on the outside, like the blurb of a novel is found on the back cover of the book. So enter this world, but never forget that you are always in charge.

THE FIVE ELEMENTS AND THE SHAPE OF YOUR BODY

WATER, fire, wood, metal and earth are the Five Chinese Elements. They exist everywhere and in everything in large or small amounts. Each one has its own characteristics, quality and shape (see page 15). In this book the term gold is used instead of metal, as it is in many Chinese texts. Gold is used because it is classically associated with immortality since it doesn't corrode, rust or fade.

This is how the Five Elements are described in the *Shu Ching*, an ancient Chinese text written more than 3000 years ago:

The first is named water; the second, fire; the third, wood; the fourth, metal; the fifth, earth. [The nature of] water is to soak and descend; of fire, to blaze and ascend; of wood, to be crooked and to be straight; of metal, to obey and to change; while the virtue of earth is seen in seed-sowing and in gathering. That which soaks and descends becomes salt;

that which blazes and ascends becomes bitter; that which is crooked and straight becomes sour; that which obeys and changes becomes acrid; and from seed sowing and ingathering comes sweetness.

Shu Ching (Book of History), trans. J. Legge

In Chinese physiognomy humans are matched up with at least one of the elements although most people are a combination of two or more. You have to find out which basic shape you correspond to and then find out which other elements occur in your appearance by taking into account your character and your build. Each of the elements is expressed in the basic shape of the body and of the hands. For example, you could be a gold person, square and strongly built; or you could be mainly gold with a hint of earth, muscular and strong with a sallow complexion. You first need to identify which element is strongest in your body by reading the main element shapes below and then see if it combines with a lesser element.

Your elemental shape is only a guide to your character. In order for a full reading to be made you would have to take into account hand lines and facial features. For example, we could say that a water-shaped person is intelligent but this is confirmed by a deep, unbroken head line on the palm of the hand (Fig 1).

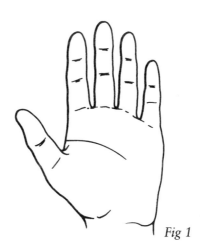

Fig 1

21

THE FIVE ELEMENTAL BODY SHAPES

Water Shape

The water-shaped person has a round body. This does not mean that you are fat but that your limbs are smoothly rounded and your bones well padded by skin. You have a calm, quiet nature and a direct, open manner. Your skin is soft, full of colour and has a slightly oily appearance. The base of your fingers should be strong, the fingertips pointed and your fingers conical in shape. Your knuckles are not bony or prominent. The head line on your palm (A) should slope downwards which is a sign of creativity and intelligence (Fig 2).

Water shape with gold

Water works well if you have some gold in your nature. You can identify gold by pale-coloured skin and a square-shaped body. A small amount of gold in the water shape is seen in a round body and a square shape and is a sign of good fortune. If the gold is too heavy for water the body is round, the face square and the voice high and sharp. The skin is white, the bones of the body can be seen and the veins stand out. The forecast for this shape is not so positive. You will need patience and hard work to achieve your goals. It is traditionally said that too much gold muddies the clarity of water.

The correct balance for this combination of water and gold can be seen if you have patches of white on a darker skin. You have what is known as a square nature which means you sit calmly and act slowly and methodically.

Water shape with earth

This mixture is seen in someone with a dry, yellow complexion. You are likely to suffer from regular minor illnesses and short

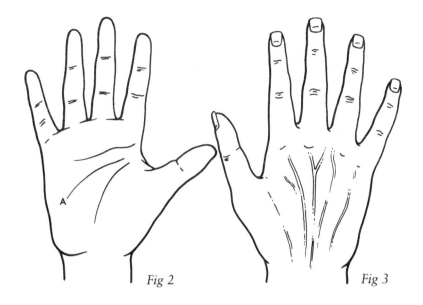

Fig 2   Fig 3

bouts of bad luck. If there are only slight tinges of yellow on the skin and a glossy complexion the reading is much improved.

Water shape with fire or wood

Red skin colouring is an indication of the fire element and tinges of green are an indication of the wood nature. Both combine very well with water.

Fire Shape

The fire-shaped person has a long head, wide chin and a domed forehead. Your face is red and shiny and your hair is brown or red. Your ears are slightly pointed and the eyebrows rise upwards. The bones and sinews on your hands and face can be seen easily and your voice is usually dry and rough. Your hands are strong and have a sharp appearance (Fig 3).

You have a well-mannered nature but your hot temper explodes if you are pushed. You are best suited to disciplined, orderly work and are likely to be successful before middle age, although you may lose power or authority unexpectedly. Just as fire flares quickly but eventually subsides, your fortune throughout life will fluctuate. Wealth and happiness may suddenly arrive, fade away and then return unexpectedly. Your best elemental combination is wood, since wood fuels the fire and keeps the flames bright.

Fire shape with wood

A sign of this combination is a clear voice, a thin straight body and a well-defined bone structure. It is a positive combination which denotes success or fame from the age of thirty onwards.

Fire shape with water

These two elements are not compatible since water extinguishes fire. This combination is identified in a round build and dark complexion; if you are looking at the body the bones and the sinews are not well defined. You are likely to have an emotionally unpredictable relationship with a partner or your children and find it hard to save money.

Fire shape with earth

Yellow skin colouring and a strong build, particularly across the shoulders and the back, are a sign of fire with earth. It is traditionally said that since fire produces earth, earth has less strength and energy than a pure fire nature, but this is still a good combination. The qualities of the fire person are present but in smaller quantities.

Fire shape with gold

This is an unusual combination, and it is difficult to identify pale tinges to the skin and the square shape associated with gold against the dominant fire element. It is more common and easier to find a gold-shaped person with a fire nature.

Wood Shape

A wood-shaped person is thin, tall and straight, with strong hard joints and sinews. Your eyes are long and clear and your eyebrows are thick. At certain times your skin may appear to have a green tinge. Your waist is slim in relation to your build and your feet are flat and long. The skin over the joints of your hands has a knotted appearance and your fingers and toes are long. When you examine the hands, it is not unusual to find many small, vertical lines on the skin. the true wood-shaped person has a kind nature and is sympathetic to the misfortune of others. You can expect a long and stable life (Fig 4).

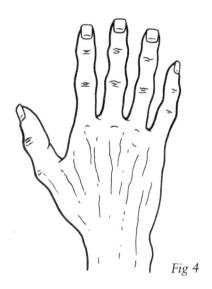

Fig 4

Wood shape with gold

The body is squarely built and the skin has golden tinges. Someone with this combination will have difficulty achieving financial rewards even though they put in considerable time and effort. If there is only a small amount of gold in your shape you may be able to mould this so that the best qualities of the wood shape emerge.

Wood shape with water

This is the luckiest combination to have with wood since, according to the Chinese tradition regarding elements, water produces wood. If you have this combination you are likely to have a natural artistic skill, and as long as the water element is not too strong many opportunities will come your way. The water element can be identified if parts of your body are thicker, plumper or more rounded.

Wood shape with fire

This combination is recognised in a red face and moist or greasy skin. The growing pattern of fire is similar to that of wood which makes this a positive and lucky mixture.

Wood shape with earth

This combination is usually recognised by a mixture of yellow and green tinges in the skin and raised veins on the hands. You are likely to have a strong build but earth reduces the power of wood which may weaken your health and give you less patience than a true wood-shaped person.

Gold Shape

The gold-shaped person has a square build and a brightness in their complexion. The body is strong boned and the muscles hard and well formed. Your facial features should be well balanced, your hands and fingers strong and square in shape (Fig 5).

You have a strong-minded, sensible, patient nature and do not change plans or break agreements. You worry about work and your concern preoccupies you in your free time. You have good powers of concentration and rarely waste your time daydreaming. You have a reliable nature, you can be trusted to keep a promise and you never forget a favour. You work hard, abide by the rules and do not tolerate mistakes made by your-

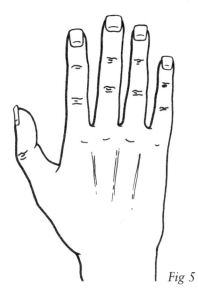

Fig 5

self or others. This combination of characteristics can create resentment amongst your colleagues. Outside work you are more tolerant, relaxed and friendly although there are times when your straightforward, honest nature can appear too abrupt.

You are suited to a career in the law or the armed forces since this will provide the order and discipline you need.

Gold shape with fire

Fire has the power to destroy gold and in this combination fire can seriously weaken the gold-shaped person. This mixture of elements can be recognised in red skin, prominent facial features and a well-defined bone structure. It is a sign that you should take care of your health and avoid situations which put you at physical risk. If there are only slight tinges of red in the skin you have a light fire nature and are able to mould circumstances to your benefit, just as fire can mould gold. From the age of forty onwards you are likely to enter a prosperous and happy stage in your life.

Gold shape with earth

This is a lucky combination since earth produces gold. You may be successful in a career which involves trading or planning, but whichever job you choose it may not be long before your work produces financial rewards. Gold shape with earth is identified in a well-built frame, firm muscles and yellow skin colouring. Too much earth in your nature can detract from this reading since earth can prevent gold from being discovered.

Gold shape with water

It is rare to see this combination and hard to identify because of the dominant gold element. When this combination appears it is a sign of good fortune although you are more likely to see a water-shaped person with a gold nature.

Gold shape with wood

Since the gold shape is seen in a large build and the wood in a thin one, it is hard to recognise this combination except in the hands. The sinews and veins can be clearly seen and the knuckles are bony. It denotes a hard working life and difficulty attaining promotion or developing your career.

Earth Shape

The earth-shaped person has large and thickset features. You have a large mouth and nose, thick lips, round chin, hard muscles and strong bones. Your skin colour has a golden/yellow tinge and your voice is strong and loud. Your hands are likely to be thick, rounded, powerful and muscular (Fig 6).

Even under the most difficult circumstances you are honest, loyal, trusting and hardworking. You put effort into your work but it is unlikely that you will ever be famous or wealthy. You have a truthful nature and can be relied upon to keep a promise.

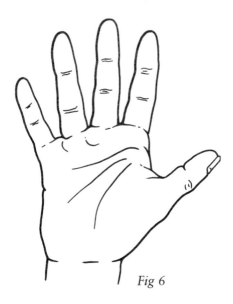

Fig 6

It is hard for others to guess what you are thinking, but if you feel strongly about an issue you are not afraid to speak your mind. You are full of energy, skilful in your actions and adept at planning.

Earth shape with wood

The elements of earth and wood jar against each other. This combination is recognised by veins which can be seen through the skin and a green tinge to the complexion. You are likely to find it hard to make or save money, and many of your schemes and ideas do not work out as planned.

Earth shape with fire

This is a positive combination since fire warms the earth and helps it to maintain life. You can identify this mixture by looking closely at the skin which should have a yellow tinge with red colouring underneath. It denotes a successful and lucky life.

Earth shape with water

This is a rare combination but is identified in dark skin colouring and a traditional earth shape. A reading for this mixture advises you to be patient with your family and colleagues and to be prepared for unexpected disappointments.

Earth shape with gold

This combination is recognised in a large build and white to yellow skin colouring. Since earth produces gold this is a lucky combination that promises success and wealth.

2

ANIMAL SHAPES

YOU CAN TAKE a reading from the body according to the Five Elemental Shapes in Chapter 1 or according to the shape of twenty-five different animals. In traditional Chinese physiognomy a resemblance to a particular animal in the way we move, look or speak can bestow on us certain qualities associated with that animal. There are times when it is difficult to know why someone is fortunate in life and the answer according to Chinese physiognomy could be that they resemble an animal associated with good fortune, wealth or fame.

Phoenix Shape

The eyes are narrow and long and there is no eyelid. The nose is curved, the eyes are clear and the chin and the lower cheeks are narrow. The body is long and slight, the walk is elegant and the voice clear.

You have a bright, alert character and a sensitivity to the world around you. You also have a creative nature and are likely to be a skilled writer or artist. You are well respected by colleagues and friends alike.

Eagle Shape

The head is square but the forehead is round and wide. The eyebrows are thick and the eyes bright and round with tinges of yellow and red in the iris. The mouth is small but the lips are full and pursed.

You are cautious and alert but when you decide to act you respond decisively and quickly. You are not afraid of challenge or combat and it is this drive that earns you respect and admiration.

Crane Shape

The eyebrows slope downwards, the cheekbones are prominent, the cheeks themselves are thin and hollowed and the chin is narrow. The nose is sharp, thin and high, and the neck is long and thin. The overall shape of the body is thin and when walking the stride is wide.

You have an intelligent and interested approach to life and are capable of achieving a responsible career. Although the chance of fame or wealth may come your way you are not ambitious and would be content with a quiet, peaceful life.

Goose Shape

The nose turns inwards at the tip and the mouth and eyes are small. The body is long but the legs are short. The body movements are slow and deliberate so that each action happens gradually and seems to be thought out beforehand.

You do not need continual reassurance or support and usually accept the circumstances or environment that surrounds you. Your forethought and deliberation are likely to pay off and you can expect a comfortable lifestyle.

Magpie Shape

The face is small, the ears are high on the head and the skin has a greenish-white tinge. The walk is brisk and the voice clear.

You choose your words carefully before you speak.

You are a good orator and people enjoy listening to your descriptions or explanations of events. You are admired and respected for your judgement and knowledge which you are happy to share with others.

Duck Shape

The body is well-rounded, the mouth is small and the legs are short. You usually walk at a slow pace.

You have a winning character that draws others to you. Wherever you go your outgoing nature enables you to make friends easily. It seems that you have a lucky life and you make the most of it through your enjoyment of food, drink and good company.

Pigeon Shape

The overall frame of the body is small, as are the facial features. The eyes are alert and have a greenish-red tinge.

You have a restless character and before long your attention is caught by someone or something and you are off to investigate. You also enjoy singing and are often heard humming away to yourself. You are content with life but if you are thinking of setting up in business you would be advised to choose someone with a good head for financial matters.

Partridge Shape

The skin has a reddish tinge and the iris is marked with red and yellow tinges. The body and the ears are small. You look at the floor when you are walking and your head moves from side to side.

You put effort into your work but sometimes fortune seems to be working against you. It may take a long time for you to establish yourself and find a stable income but with perseverance you can achieve this.

Mandarin-Duck Shape

The skin has a pinkish tinge and the eyes are slightly upturned at the corner. Your footsteps are uneven in length and the walk is usually jerky.

You are more likely to plan ahead than act erratically or on impulse. You have a flirtatious character and often seek out the company of the opposite sex. You trust your friends and rely on them to help you sort out difficulties in your domestic or social life.

Crow Shape

The face is round, the nose is large and the lips are pursed. The eyes are dark with a hint of green.

You enjoy conversation and debate but once you start you find it hard to stop. You become so involved with discussions that you fail to recognise that others may have heard enough.

Dragon Shape

The build is strong and powerful and the bones are large. The eyebrows are thick and rise upwards and the eyes are clear. The walk is determined and steady and the face looks composed and reliable.

You are a trustworthy and honest character and it is rare for you to act foolishly or erratically. You have a strong character and although you relate well to others and appreciate their company you are not the sort of person who will suddenly burst out laughing or make a meaningless remark. Your thoughts and actions are considered and intelligent. According to Chinese physiognomy this shape is rarely seen.

Lion Shape

The forehead is high, the nose and eyes large and the head is square. The hair is thick and strong. The bones on the back of the head are well developed and prominent. (This area of the head is called the 'pillow stone' since it is the first part of the head to touch the pillow.)

You know how to judge a situation and are unlikely to make a decision until you have examined all relevant aspects. This ability to assess events and act accordingly is admired by others who often come to you for advice and guidance.

Elephant Shape

The eyebrows are high and grow beyond the eyetail and the forehead is wide. The ears are large and do not usually have rings or wheels (see Chapter 9). The nose is upturned and the lips curl outwards slightly so the teeth can be seen. The body is well built and muscular and the movements are steady and deliberate.

You have a natural empathy for others and will be there for them when they need you. You have a generous nature and are happy to share your time or personal possessions. It is unusual for anyone to take advantage of your generosity and for the most part what you give is appreciated.

Gibbon Shape

The face and features are round and small, the lips are pursed and the voice is loud. The arms are usually longer than the legs and the body is thin although the cheeks and chin are fleshy and plump.

You have a sensitive nature and are easily hurt but there is also a side to your character that is preoccupied with the way you look and dress. You like to check your appearance regularly, frequently brushing your hair or washing your face and hands. Your actions are swift and organised and you are suited to a disciplined job.

Monkey Shape

The cheekbones are high and the eyes are deep set and round. The complexion is tinged with yellow and red and the nose and ears are set high on the face. Although the gestures tend to be unsteady, the movements are lively and unpredictable.

You are alert and observant to life around you. You are also deeply affected by emotional upsets or when you see unnecessary suffering. You do what you can to respond to these distressing situations but you sometimes lack confidence and courage.

Tortoise Shape

The head is dome shaped, the eyes are round, the eyebrows are thick and the nose is set high on the face. You have a round jaw, long neck and thick shoulders. The body is fat and round and the Five Mountains (see Chapter 4) of the face are well balanced.

You have a relaxed and peaceful attitude to life. When those around you get excited or angry you usually maintain a calm disposition. You work on the principle that there is no point becoming upset since it will not solve the problem. You like to work at a steady, calm pace which gives you a chance to think through the problem and find solutions.

Snake Shape

The forehead is narrow, the eyebrows are small and the nose is short and sharp. The eyes are long in shape and muddy green in colour. The lips are usually pursed and the teeth are sharp. The ears are small, wide at the top, narrow at the bottom, and there is little or no pearl (see Chapter 9). The waist is wide and the flesh feels soft. When you walk you move slightly from side to side instead of walking in a straight line.

You do not boast about your strengths or reveal your weaknesses since privacy and secrecy are important to you. Sometimes you appear not to be concentrating but you are usually well aware of what is happening around you. There are times when you lose patience and respond sharply or critically.

Cow Shape

The body is strong and sturdy, the head is large and the neck is powerful. The mouth is large and the lips sometimes appear to be moving slightly even though you are not speaking. The iris of the eye is large, bright and black. You usually walk slowly.

You are thoughtful and kind towards friends and strangers. If help is needed you are usually there to lend a hand or offer words of support. Your natural friendliness is a positive characteristic that will take you far in your working life.

Horse Shape

The body and the face are long, the eyes and mouth are large, and the teeth are strong and wide. Your actions are slow and steady whether you are walking or sitting.

You have good common sense and usually act with consideration and thought but there are times when you can be impetuous and rash. Your determination is generally respected as is your normally calm nature.

Lamb Shape

The face is long but the forehead cannot be seen clearly because it is narrow or covered by hair. The chin is thin and the lips are pursed. A lamb-shaped man is likely to have a small beard. The eyes are muddy yellow and the iris is small. Your legs are usually short and when walking you look down at the floor.

You have a pleasant, outgoing and trustworthy character. You are not likely to let unexpected events or setbacks disturb your outlook and usually find a way to resolve the problem. You are well liked by friends and colleagues and are willing to take responsibility for your work and your actions.

Pig Shape

The head is large, the face is long and the forehead is flat. The eyes are deep set, the lips are pursed and the ears are slightly pointed. Your neck and legs are short.

You have an easy-going outlook on life and are happy to let the time pass in conversation with friends. You also have an extravagant nature and enjoy spending money on other people as well as yourself.

Rat Shape

The complexion has a deep red tinge and the eyes are round. Your expression is alert and your movements are cautious. You behave in a secretive way, even preferring to eat your food on your own.

You are sensitive and easily hurt by a chance remark or action. You are wary of the world around you and before you agree to a suggestion you like to be given all the necessary details to prepare yourself.

Rabbit Shape

All the facial features except for the ears are small. Your nose is slightly red and you have many teeth which grow close together.

You have a creative nature and are likely to be interested in design and colour. You have exciting ideas and plans going on in your head and are full of imagination. Others are attracted by your openness and creativity.

Camel Shape

The head is round, the face and neck are long and the forehead is wide. The skin around the eyes is thick, the eyebrows are rough and the mouth is pursed. The shoulders, legs and arms are powerful and the voice is loud and resonant.

You are a reliable and trustworthy friend and colleague. If you are asked for help you rarely refuse and will do what is required of you efficiently and quickly. Your attitude to work is also thorough and your ambition is to be successful in your career. You are capable of achieving this.

3

THE HANDS

THE LINES on your hands are continually changing and growing so the reading they provide differs at each stage of your life.

According to Chinese palmistry a woman's right hand and a man's left hand reflect their actions, thoughts, aspirations and fortune. This is the hand that we guide, influence and alter according to the pattern of our life and our personality. The opposite hand – in this case a woman's left hand and a man's right hand – is the hand that is influenced by family and inherited characteristics. It is said to be the hand we are born with. The right and the left hand have their own responsibilities and one does not control the other.

When you are taking a reading and you want to look at the past, present and future in relation to your personality you should take a reading from the right hand if you are female and the left hand if you are male. Stretch your hand out fully so the lines can be seen clearly.

THE IDEAL HAND

Ideally, the size of the hand should be in proportion with the rest of the body although a disproportionately larger hand is considered luckier than a smaller hand. The skin should have elasticity and not be too soft or smooth since this is seen as a sign of laziness. Hard, strong hands which are fleshy enough to hide the bones are a sign that you can spot a good business venture and have a skill for making money. The fingers and the thumb should be strong and straight and the palm of the hand should be firm but fleshy with well-defined lines (see Fig 7 which shows a traditional Chinese drawing of the 'ideal' hand).

Bright pinky red or yellow colouring indicates good 'ch'i' or energy in your hands whereas dry, grey skin lacks a healthy flow of ch'i.

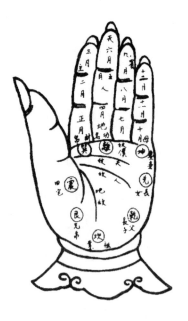

Fig 7

The Shape and Feel of the Hand

A thick, soft hand and a powerful thumb are a sign of long life (although this should be checked against the life line, see Fig 8 below). A weak thumb, thin hand and soft papery skin are a sign of weak health. Short, weak, stumpy thumbs and badly-shaped hands do not necessarily mean bad luck and before any conclusions are drawn you should check the readings to match the lines on your hand.

THE LINES ON THE HAND

There are, on average, thirty lines on a hand and six are used as the basis for reading a hand. They are the life line, head line, heart line, career line, success line and marriage line. Of these, the most influential are the head, heart and life lines; the others are subordinate (Fig 8).

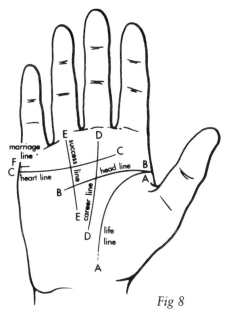

Fig 8

There are also many features on the lines, most of which are easily distinguished and which have special names, such as 'star', 'island', 'chain' and 'mountain'. Their position, height, length or depth on the hand affect the overall reading.

Stars

The palm of the hand is divided into eight areas which are referred to as 'stars'. The stars form a boundary around the centre of the palm. The centre itself is known as the 'five stars field' (Fig 9).

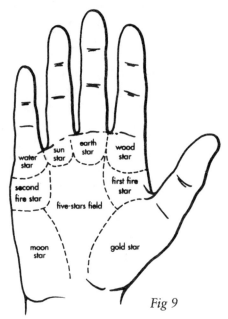

Fig 9

Islands

An island is a round or oval-shaped loop which can occur at any point on the length of a line (Fig 10).

Fig 10

Chains

A chain is a line which has links or loops along all or part of its length (Fig 11).

Fig 11

Mountains

There are five mountains on the hand. Three are the round mounds of flesh at the base of the fingers and two are the mounds of flesh at the base of the palm, on either side (Fig 12).

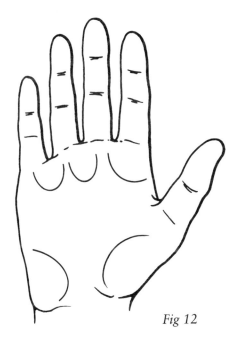

Fig 12

THE EIGHT TRIGRAMS – HOW TO FIND THEM ON THE HAND

Yin and yang are dynamic forces that keep our universe in a constant state of change. They are opposites that work in tension with one another and their constant interaction gives rise to new life, to the changes of the seasons, and to the pattern of our own mental and physical wellbeing. Yang is hot, fiery and heavy, the force in the sun, storms, fire and earth. Yin is light and cool, the force in the moon, air and water. As one begins to grow and ascend the other declines, and so they continually form a wave of movement, rising and falling in relation to one another.

In the ancient Chinese divination system of the *I Ching*, yin and yang can be symbolically represented as lines. Yang is a straight line (—) and yin is a broken line (--). When they are put in a set of three they are known as a trigram and there are eight possible combinations. These trigrams correspond to areas of the hand and each trigram has a particular image and traditional meaning in Chinese (Fig 13):

TRIGRAM	IMAGE	MEANING IN PHYSIOGNOMY
Ch'ien	Heaven	Father and elder son
K'un	Earth	Mother and elder daughter
Chen	Thunder	Education
K'an	Water	Inheritance
Ken	Mountain	Brothers
Sun	Wind, wood	Wealth
Li	Fire	Fame
Tui	Marsh	Wife, mistress and children

The eight trigrams can be understood as images of everything that happens in heaven and on earth. They are in a continual state of change just as everything in our lives is constantly changing.

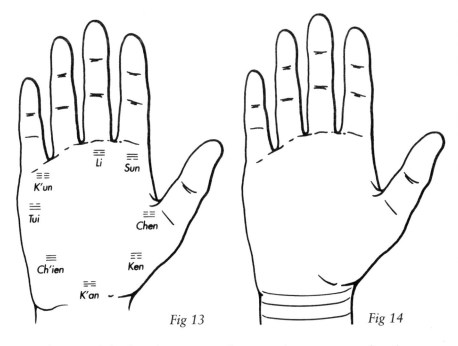

Fig 13

Fig 14

Each star of the hand corresponds to a trigram except for the sun star and the first fire star.

STAR	TRIGRAM
Gold star	Chen and Ken
Wood star	Sun
Earth star	Li
Water star	K'un
Second fire star	Tui
Moon star	Ch'ien

In addition to these positions there is also a trigram on the lower middle palm which is known as K'an.

Your fortune is affected by the shape, colour and size of each star. Smooth, fleshy skin with several well-defined lines is a positive sign but stars that are too lined or too flat give a negative reading. Three horizontal lines below K'an are known as the 'three star line' and indicate wealth, success in your career and a long life (Fig 14). Many people have these lines but they should be well-formed and straight.

45

Reading the lines on your hand

The life, head and heart lines are the main lines to consider for a hand reading. They should be long, clear, deep and interrupted as little as possible by chains or islands. They should be neither too deep nor too wide. The head, heart and life lines cover a life span of seventy years and are divided into sections to cover different ages (figs. 15 and 16).

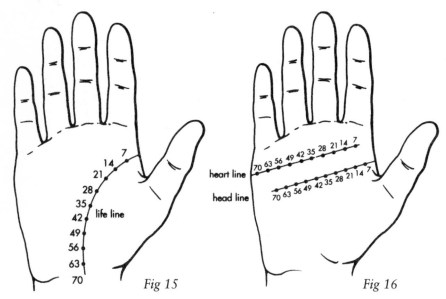

Fig 15   Fig 16

The Life Line

There are three types of life line. The readings listed below under 'Points to look for' can be applied to any of the life lines. The life lines are:

1   From the bottom of the gold star to the area between the first finger and thumb (Fig 17).

2   From the middle of the hand to the area between the first finger and thumb (Fig 18).

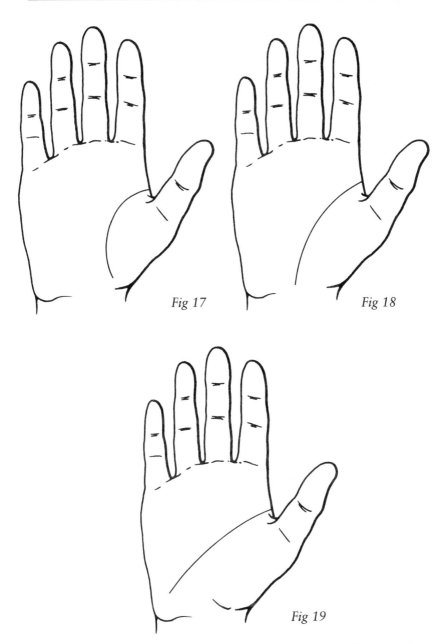

Fig 17

Fig 18

Fig 19

3   From the moon star to the area between the first finger and thumb (Fig 19).

POINTS TO LOOK FOR:

- If any part of the life line is uneven, crossed or faint, it is known as a rough line and indicates periods of upheaval in your life.

- A deep, long, dark-red life line combined with a hard hand, rough skin and well-rounded gold star is a sign that you like physical contact or dangerous activities.

- If the gold star is flat and the life line curves around its bottom edge, you will have weak health. The shape is also seen as a sign of greed.

- A thin life line that is difficult to see is a sign of poor health and recurrent illness, but the reading is improved if the thumb is straight, the hand thick and hard and the head line clear and strong.

- If you have a short life line or no life line you could still live to old age but may suffer serious sickness or face dangerous risks.

- A hooked life line on both hands is a sign of a severe illness or accident at the age where it breaks away (Fig 20). The same reading is given to a broken life line on one hand and a straight life line on the other.

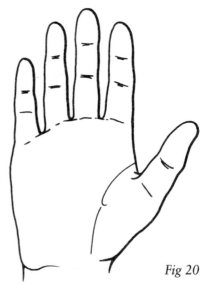

- If the life line branches but then continues as normal you may have an unexpected accident or sickness, but help will arrive in time.

Fig 20

The Head Line

The head line is an indicator of health and longevity and is thought to be just as important as, if not more important than, the life line. A deep, well-formed, unbroken head line is a sign of intelligence.

POINTS TO LOOK FOR:

- If the head line slopes downwards you enjoy the company of friends and have a creative nature. You are suited to a career in the arts or academia (Fig 21, line A).

- A longer than average head line indicates a concern for money and an eagerness to gain material rewards. You are suited to a career in commerce (Fig 21, line B).

- A head line that rises towards the little finger is a sign of a thrifty nature. You rarely allow anything or anybody to prevent you saving or earning more money. You are suited to a career in the armed forces, the police or politics (Fig 21, line C).

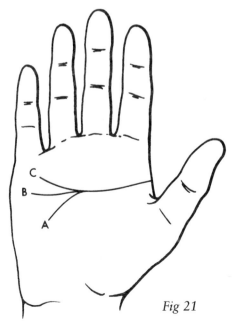

Fig 21

- If your head line is broken at a point in line with the middle finger you could have a serious accident between the ages of thirty and forty (Fig 22).

- A break in the head line on one hand but not on the other suggests emotional problems or a head injury between the ages of thirty and forty. It must be remembered that the lines are only an indicator of what may happen to you. The decisions you make and your attitude towards others can change your fate (see page 12).

- If the head line is broken in two but the lines in the gap form a square, someone in an influential position will help you in times of trouble (Fig 23).

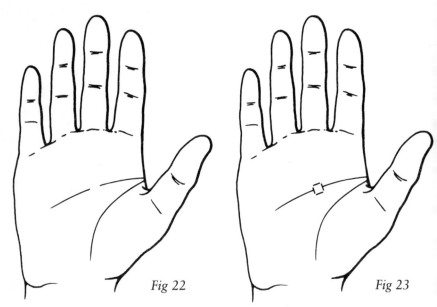

Fig 22   Fig 23

The Heart Line

The position of the heart line can determine the happiness and stability of a marriage. If you just want to know about romance you should focus on this line.

POINTS TO LOOK FOR:

- A heart line which reaches the middle of the earth star is an indication that you will pursue a romantic partner until you secure a commitment from them. Even when you are in a secure relationship you are likely to be a possessive partner (Fig 24).

- If the heart line grows to a point between the first and second finger, between the wood and earth stars, you are not interested in your partner's past. All that matters is sincerity and the strength of your relationship (Fig 25, line A).

- A heart line which points towards the wood star is a sign of powerful emotions and honesty. The efforts that you make in this relationship will probably be matched by your partner (Fig 25, line B).

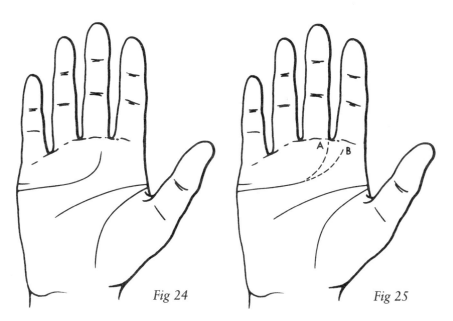

Fig 24   Fig 25

- A heart line which grows between the thumb and the first finger is a sign of deep and powerful emotions combined with a jealous streak (Fig 26, line A).

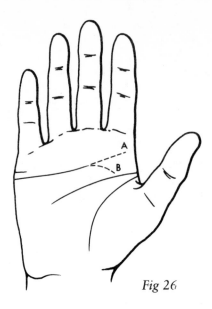

Fig 26

- If the heart line forks down towards the head line you need and enjoy the experience of many relationships. Without them life, for you, seems dull (Fig 26, line B).

CAREER, SUCCESS AND MARRIAGE LINES

Clear and unblemished career, success and marriage lines that appear alongside faint or irregular head, heart and life lines are likened to a well without a source or a tree without a root. Strong foundations are needed to support success and fame, or wealth may be short-lived.

The hand shape and the head, heart and life lines are the foundations and walls of the house, and the career, success and marriage lines are the roof.

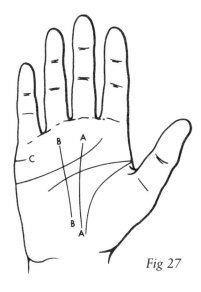

Fig 27

These are classic positions for the career (A), success (B), and marriage (C) lines, although they can appear at different positions on the hand and, in some cases, they do not appear at all.

Career line

POINTS TO LOOK FOR:

- A career line which begins at the base of the wrist and stops in the middle of the hand is a sign of difficulties and upheavals in childhood and later life (Fig 28 overleaf). This reading is improved if the mountains on the hand are high and rounded: you will be given the support you need in youth and early adulthood although you may have to face problems alone in later years.

- A career line which starts in the middle of the hand and travels up to the middle finger, combined with well-defined head, heart and life lines, indicates success and good fortune in later life (Fig 29 overleaf).

- A career line which starts in the middle of the hand and travels up to the middle finger, combined with uneven or

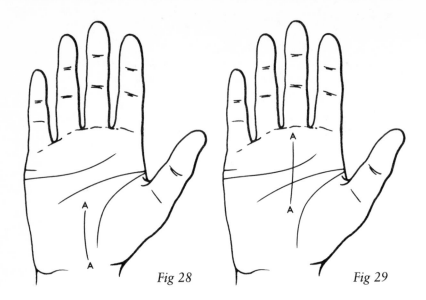

Fig 28   Fig 29

irregular mountains, is a sign of financial instability until middle age but circumstances will improve from then on.

- A career line which begins at the head line is a sign that good career opportunities will present themselves around the age of forty (Fig 30).

- If the career line is broken in the middle but there is an additional line running alongside this break (Fig 31), you are likely to have a change of business or career. If this additional line is straighter and clearer at the top than the bottom, your change in career will be an improvement on your previous position.

- A career line which is broken and lacks a covering parallel line is a sign of unemployment or lack of job security (Fig 32).

- The Chinese say that someone who has a career line leading directly from the gold star is 'drowning in enjoyment'. This is a sign of indulgence, particularly if the gold star is thick and prominent (Fig 33).

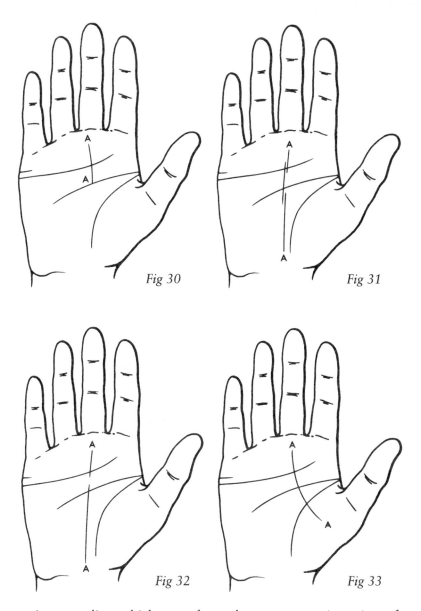

Fig 30

Fig 31

Fig 32

Fig 33

- A career line which runs from the moon star is a sign of success in business partnerships (Fig 34 overleaf). When you most need support someone usually appears to help. This type of career line is also a sign that you may marry young.

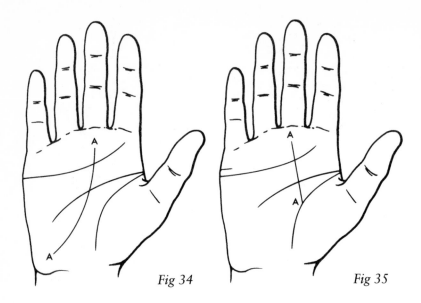

Fig 34   *Fig 35*

- A career line which runs from the moon star is considered a good career line for a woman since a husband or partner will offer strong support. If a man has this career line combined with straight, unbroken head, heart and life lines he is likely to be successful in the arts as a writer, actor, composer or artist. Also, this combination is often seen on the hand of someone writing or speaking on religious issues.

- If your career line branches directly from your life line you are likely to have established a business or career through your own vision, efforts and hard work (Fig 35). If the career line is broken at any point along its length, then your job is likely to change or to finish.

- If your career line grows to a point at the side of the hand between the thumb and the first finger, you should be careful not to put your job in jeopardy because of your moods or hot temper (Fig 36).

- An island at the beginning of the career line denotes career upheavals or obstacles in early adulthood (Fig 37, point A).

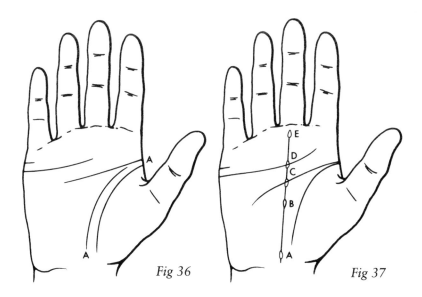

Fig 36   Fig 37

If both hands have an island at the beginning of the life line it is a sign of a fickle nature.

- An island in the middle of the career line denotes a difficult period in your career or business (Fig 37, point B).

- An island at the point where head and career lines meet indicates loss of business through bad planning or ill-advised judgement (Fig. 37, point C).

- An island at the junction of career and heart lines means loss of business through an emotional upset involving a spouse or a partner (Fig 37, point D).

- An island at the end of the career line is a sign of a sudden decline or loss of business even though trade or orders may have been flourishing (Fig 37, point E).

- Short lines crossing the career line are a sign of problems or setbacks during that particular period of your life (Fig 38, points A and B, overleaf).

- A cross at the top of the career line is an indication of illness (Fig 38, point C, overleaf).

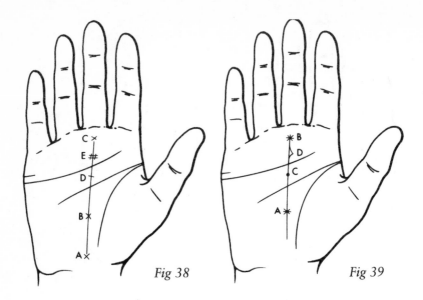

Fig 38   Fig 39

- A sharp line crossing the career line marks the point in your life when you may unexpectedly lose money or your job (Fig 38, point D).

- If a set of lines crossing your career line forms a box someone will arrive with financial help in a time of need. It is traditionally known as a 'noble square' (Fig 38, point E).

- A star crossing the career line is a sign of wealth (Fig 39, point A) but a star at the top of the career line signifies illness (Fig 39, point B).

- A dark spot on the career line is an indication of business failure (Fig 39, point C).

- A triangle on the career line marks a period of promotion or increased profits (Fig 39, point D).

- If your career line is broken in many places, you have difficulty settling in any one job and find it difficult to establish a pattern in your working life (Fig 40).

- A wavy career line is an indication of a frequent succession of job or career changes (Fig 41).

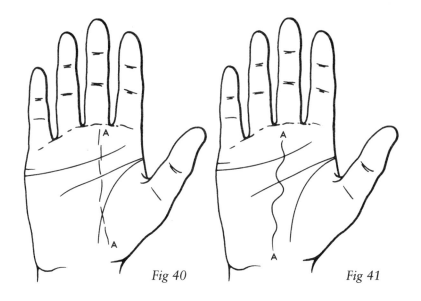

Fig 40   Fig 41

The Success Line

The success line is linked to the career line and is an indicator of your career progress. If you have a distinct career line but lack a success line you may lack job satisfaction although you have a well-established and profitable career.

A success line without a career line is a sign of easily acquired wealth but it may come from a questionable source. The career and success lines are influential and it is better to have none than have ones that are badly broken or irregular.

The ideal success line (A) is straight, deep and thin. It stretches from the base of the hand up to the third finger (sun star). When this is combined with a straight, well-defined career line (B) it promises good fortune and financial security throughout your working life (Fig 42 overleaf). You should only take readings from one success line. Choose the longest or the most clearly formed. The appearance of two or three success lines on your hand does not mean that you will be two or three times as successful.

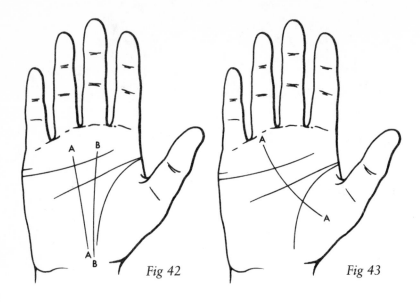

Fig 42

Fig 43

POINTS TO LOOK FOR:

- If your success line reaches from the gold star to the sun star you will probably enjoy a happy and prosperous family life (Fig 43).

- A success line which travels from the moon star to the sun star is a sign of success in partnerships; it is also an indicator of a reliable colleague or friend offering support during difficult times (Fig 44).

- If the success line grows from the head line your career progress is due to your own hard work and well-developed plans (Fig 45). This success line must be combined with a well-developed career line.

- If the success line branches straight from the heart line you may not be successful in a career or in business until middle age (Fig 46). When this line is clear and straight it indicates fame in the arts or a creative field.

- A success line that leads straight from the life line to the sun star is a sign of business success which is initially marred by setbacks or failures (Fig 47). A straight career line combined

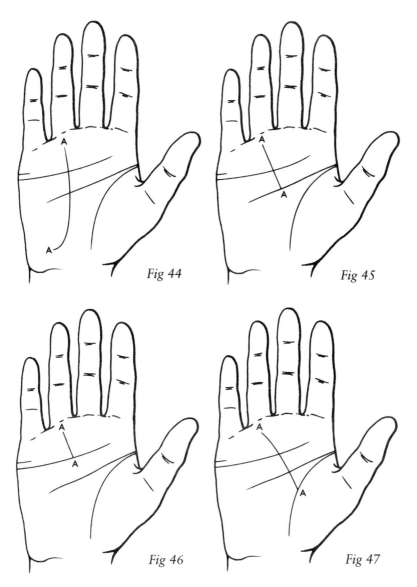

Fig 44

Fig 45

Fig 46

Fig 47

with a success line leading from the second fire star to the sun star is a reference to a disciplined nature. You would, for example, be suited to a career in the armed forces. If you also have lines forming a star in the area of the wood star you are likely to attain a position or rank of authority.

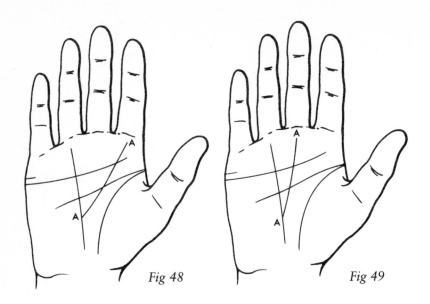

Fig 48   Fig 49

- A line branching off the success line to the wood star is a sign that you may be offered a promotion when you least expect it (Fig 48).

- If your success line branches off the career line and up to the earth star you may be offered a job with good career possibilities but you will unexpectedly suffer a career setback or loss (Fig 49).

- If your career line forks towards the water star you are likely to be gifted in commerce or science and will achieve recognition for your work in your lifetime (Fig 50).

- A wavy success line denotes hard work but little success, and a grey or white success line will give the same reading (Fig 51).

- A success line which stops in the middle of the hand is a sign of success in your early career, but by middle age your career may go into decline (Fig 52).

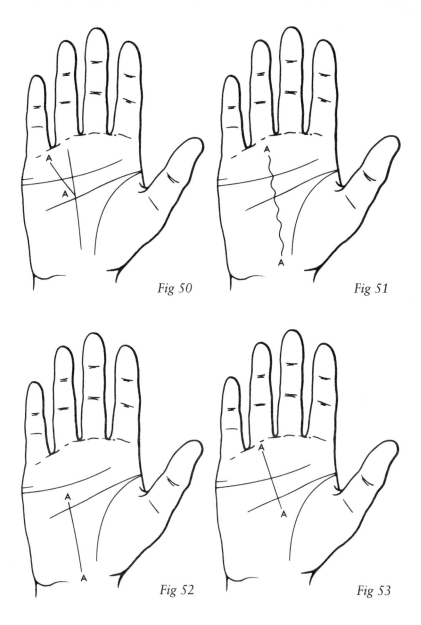

Fig 50

Fig 51

Fig 52

Fig 53

- A success line which starts in the middle of the hand and grows towards the sun star is a sign of career difficulties leading up to middle age but success afterwards (Fig 53).

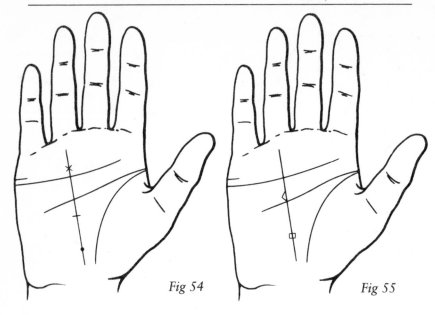

Fig 54

Fig 55

- If your success line is cut by a small line, cross or black spot you could be entering a period of setbacks and misfortune but it will eventually pass (Fig 54).

- A triangle or square on the success line is a lucky omen; someone will come to your help in times of need (Fig 55). A star on the success line is also a lucky sign whereas a star on the career line is considered unlucky.

MARRIAGE LINES

These lines reveal whether your love is likely to be true, long lasting, blessed by good fortune or not. They also indicate the approximate year of marriage, its length and its stability.

Age at Marriage

The marriage line is found above the heart line, in the area of the water star. You may have two or three marriage lines which vary in length. You should take a reading from the longest, straightest line.

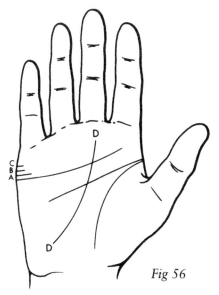

Fig 56

POINTS TO LOOK FOR:

- If the longest, straightest line is closest to the heart line, you should marry between the ages of eighteen and twenty-four (Fig 56, line A).

- A line in the middle position signifies marriage between the ages of twenty-four and thirty-two years of age (Fig 56, line B).

- The line nearest the base of the little finger indicates marriage from the age of thirty-two (Fig 56, line C).

- If the lines are crooked or unclear you are advised to marry after the age of thirty-two. If you are planning to marry before the age indicated by your marriage line, check that your gold star is well rounded and that your career line begins at the moon star and ends at the earth star (Fig 56, line D).

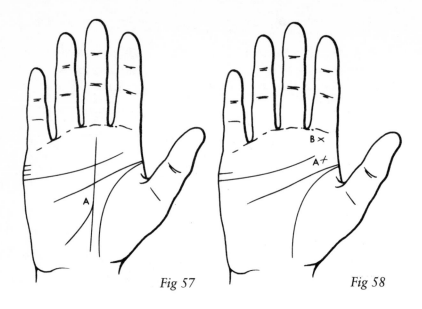

Fig 57   *Fig 58*

- The marriage line does not always control the time of your marriage. A line running from the moon star to the career line is also used as a reference. The marrying age is estimated from the point at which the two lines meet. The point at which they meet in Fig 57 is in the early thirties age group.

- Lines forming a cross in the area of the wood star also help to determine your age at marriage. Crossed lines close to the head line indicate marriage early in life (Fig 58, point A), and crossed lines close to the wood star suggest your early thirties (Fig 58, point B). Readings from these crosses usually override readings given on the marriage line.

The Marriage Line

POINTS TO LOOK FOR:

- A marriage line which slopes down to the head line is an indication of a flirtatious nature or a desire for extra-marital affairs (Fig 59, line A).

- A marriage line which slopes so far down towards the heart line that it almost touches is a sign of separation (Fig 59, line B). If this line crosses the heart line it could signify divorce.

- If the marriage line forks at the end, the marriage may begin well but end up in separation or divorce (Fig 59, line C).

- If the end of the marriage line branches out into three or more lines, difficulties or upheavals in marriage will be resolved (Fig 59, line D).

- If the career line is met at an angle by a line from the moon star and the success line rises from this angle, then the marriage will be happy and prosperous (Fig 60).

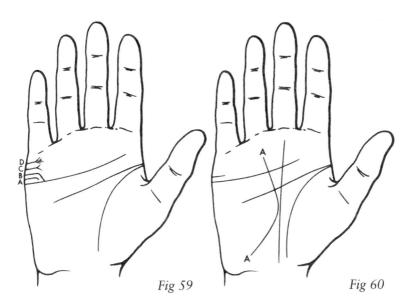

Fig 59   Fig 60

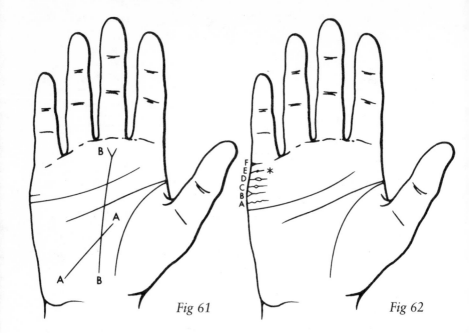

Fig 61

Fig 62

- When a line from the moon star passes straight through the career line the marriage may pass through many problems (Fig 61, line A). If the career line is also forked at its tip it is an indication that the couple will eventually find happiness together (Fig 61, line B).

- A wavy marriage line is a sign that your expectations for the marriage may be too great; perhaps you are setting yourself goals which cannot be attained (Fig 62, line A). The Chinese say, 'You see a flower in the mirror and the moon in the water.'

- A man whose marriage line forks at the edge of the hand is likely to be unfaithful to his wife before marriage but is likely to settle down afterwards (Fig 62, line B). If this fork occurs on a woman's hand there may be a stormy period in the early years of marriage.

- If the line is broken by a diamond shape there may be recurrent quarrels throughout the marriage, although they will usually be resolved quickly and amicably (Fig 62, line C).

- An island on the marriage line denotes divorce or separation (Fig 62, line D).

- A dark spot or a star at the end of the marriage line indicates the possibility of an unexpected serious illness for your partner (Fig 62, line E).

- If your marriage line is thick at the beginning and tapers to a thin point, the passion you feel at the start of a relationship will pass quickly (Fig 62, line F).

- A line which runs from the moon star to the career star is known as the effective line since it influences the quality of the marriage. If your effective line starts at the moon star, curves upwards, then suddenly cuts across to the career line, you are likely to meet a future partner when you are working or travelling away from home (Fig 63).

- If your effective line runs from the moon star up to the career line and then runs parallel to the career line, you may fall in love with someone who can never marry you (Fig 64).

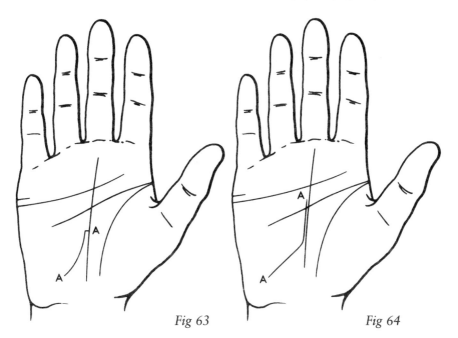

Fig 63   Fig 64

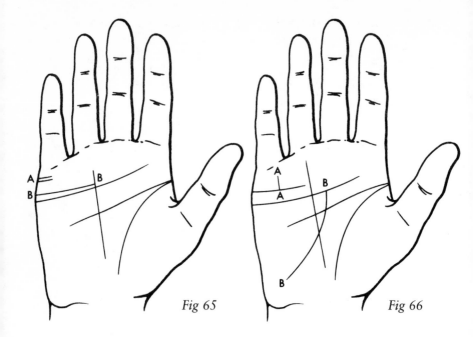

Fig 65

Fig 66

- Two marriage lines which are equally straight and long are said to indicate an affair outside marriage (Fig 65, line A).

- A marriage line which touches the success line is a sign of marriage to a wealthy partner (Fig 65, line B).

- If a small line touches the marriage line and then runs parallel to the success line you may find fame and wealth after marriage (Fig 66, line A).

- A career line that begins at the moon star and touches the heart line is a sign of a happy and contented marriage (Fig 66, line B).

- If you have a line in the area of the gold star which runs parallel to the lower life line you are likely to find a supportive and caring partner (Fig 67). If this line is broken your partner may suffer an unexpected accident (Fig 68). When an island appears along this line both partners may be unfaithful (Fig 69). If the line forks at its base there may be a divorce or separation (Fig 70).

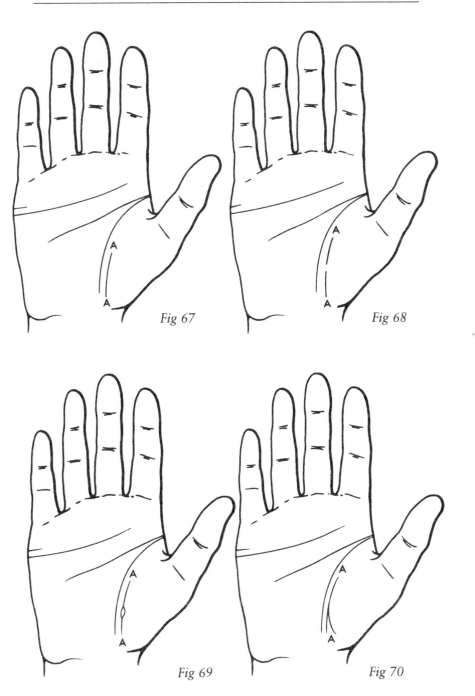

Fig 67

Fig 68

Fig 69

Fig 70

4

THE FACE

ANCIENT Chinese fortune-tellers distinguished 130 positions on the face and, over the centuries, the most important ones were put into categories.

These include the Twelve Palaces which cover different areas across the whole face, the Thirteen Positions which run in a line from the forehead to the chin, the Twelve Earthly Stems which form a circle around the face and the Three Areas of the Face which are the top, middle and lower sections of the face. There are also specific areas known as the Five Mountains and the Four Rivers.

The Thirteen Positions and the Twelve Palaces give readings up to the age of seventy and the Twelve Earthly Stems provide readings from the ages of seventy to one hundred. The Three Areas of the face give readings for youth, middle and old age and the remaining groups provide readings which are relevant at any age.

YOUR COMPLEXION

It is difficult to take a reading from the complexion unless you are experienced in physiognomy. A practitioner of Chinese physiognomy or medicine can identify the flow of ch'i which is the life force or energy. A complexion with a deep colour is a sign of strong ch'i whereas a sallow complexion is a sign of weak ch'i. Do not try to distinguish the flow of ch'i after exercise since this will have pushed the blood to the surface. The light should be soft so there are no reflections from strong sunlight or spotlights. The complexion takes various tinges which may include red, purple, green, yellow, white, black or grey.

Red is a positive colour and denotes happiness, contentment and success although deep red is considered a warning of illness or injury. Yellow is an indication of good news or the arrival of money while green can be interpreted as fear or anger. White is a sign of worry or sickness and black is also a sign of sickness and financial loss. A grey complexion is a sign of lack of attention and slow reactions. An unevenly coloured complexion is an unlucky sign and is called a 'false complexion'.

Skins that are tinged with red, yellow or purple are considered the most fortunate. Even if the skin is tinged with other colours, a healthy glow, moist skin and an animated face are a sign of active and regular ch'i.

THE THREE AREAS OF THE FACE

The face is divided into the Heavenly, Human and Earthly areas. The Heavenly area begins just below the hairline and finishes just above the ears. The Human area stretches down to

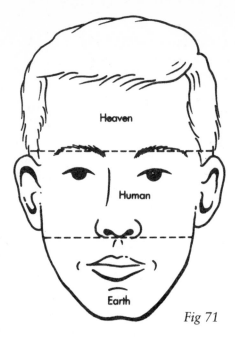

Fig 71

the tip of the nose, and the Earthly area reaches from the tip of the nose down to the chin. These three areas represent your youth, middle age and old age. It is believed that past and future events can be revealed through these areas (Fig 71).

Heavenly Area

A strong, well-developed and even Heavenly area indicates a stable and supportive family life. If the area is lumpy or the complexion dull it is a sign of an unsettled childhood. A wide forehead is a positive sign but if it is too wide in relation to the rest of the face it can detract from a good reading. This often denotes a turbulent romantic life for a woman.

Anyone who is middle-aged should have at least three lines on their forehead since this denotes a thoughtful attitude to life and a good understanding of human nature. Lines across the forehead which curve upwards signify good fortune. If the lines on your forehead are broken you may find that circumstances beyond your control keep you away from your family.

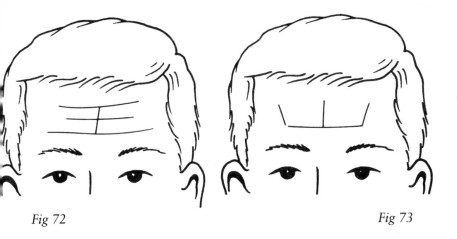

Fig 72   *Fig 73*

If the lines on your forehead form the Chinese character for 'king' (Fig 72) or for 'mountain' (Fig 73) you are likely to be respected by family and colleagues. These characters are also symbols of prosperity and good financial prospects.

The Human Area

Your nose should be well proportioned in relation to the rest of your face. If your facial features are well balanced it is a sign of a successful and prosperous middle age. Irregular features are an indication of unstable relationships during this period of your life.

If the Human area is longer than the areas above and below it you have a strong, decisive mind and are challenged by new tasks or unexpected problems. If the complexion in this area is dull and lifeless you may pass through a career change or upheavals in your working life during middle age.

The Earthly Area

If this area is well balanced in relation to the rest of your face and the bone structure even, you will have a satisfying old age. Family ties will be strong and although you may not be wealthy you are unlikely to have financial worries.

If this area is fat and the lips are thick you will still enjoy a lively romantic life, but thin lips and a narrow, bony chin are an indication of weak health.

THE THREE AREAS OF THE BODY

Just as the face is divided into three areas, the body also has the same divisions. The head to the shoulders is the Heavenly area, the shoulders to the waist is the Human area, and the waist to the toes is the Earthly area. Ideally all three should be well balanced and the Heavenly and Human areas should appear longer than the legs. Short, thin legs combined with a long, stocky body or a thin body combined with fat legs detract from a positive reading.

Feet should also be taken into account for your reading. The ideal foot has soft skin and should be wide, long and square in shape. They should not be flat or turn outwards or inwards. Lines on the sole of the foot are a sign of a healthy diet and good constitution. Eye-shaped lines signify good fortune for your family, circular lines indicate fame and a tortoiseshell pattern forecasts a prosperous life.

THE THIRTEEN POSITIONS OF THE FACE

The Thirteen Positions run from the top of the forehead to the bottom of the chin in the following order (Fig 74).

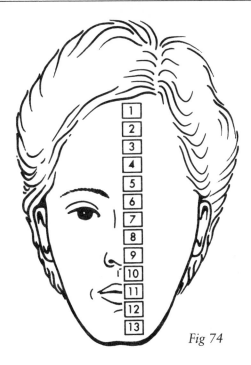

Fig 74

1. T'ien Chung

The surface of the skin should be free of cuts and the complexion clear, which is a sign of a happy youth and strong bonds with your parents. An uneven hairline or black or grey marks on the forehead indicate an unsettled childhood due to lack of money or family disagreements. Hair that grows to a point on the hairline forecasts the death of your father before that of your mother. A line that feels like a vein running up through the forehead to the hairline is said to be the shan ken (see 6) running into the forest and is a sign of an unexpected accident or failure.

2. T'ien T'ing

When you are taking a reading from this area you should also take a reading of the whole complexion. If the skin is clear, bright and unmarked you will be close to your parents and can rely on the support of an influential friend or colleague when you need help. If the skin has a grey tinge in this area it is called a 'black cloud', a sign that it is hard to convince others when you are telling the truth. A green tinge warns of an unlucky event in the next two weeks so be cautious until this colouring fades away.

3.   Ssu K'ung

If there is a yellow or red tinge on the skin it is a sign of good fortune and respect, but grey marks herald a short period of bad luck. Grey marks can appear and disappear on the skin at any time and are a warning to be patient and careful, particularly in your working life.

4.   Chung Cheng

If the area is smooth and clear it is a sign of early success in your career, but dents or an uneven surface show a lack of concentration or application to your work. A black mole or lumps in this area denote lack of patience; it is also a sign that your plans may be thwarted since you are prevented access to relevant people or places.

5.   Yin T'ang

A healthy glow in this area is a sign of a large family inheritance and good business acumen but a narrow gap between the eyebrows denotes financial setbacks. If your eyebrows meet in the middle, you cannot always be trusted.

It is said that a birth mark or scar in this area is a sign of adoption, a black mole indicates a period of illness and a black mole slightly to the side of the yin t'ang indicates legal confrontation.

Two wrinkles that run down the forehead and curve outwards towards each eye are a sign that financial or career success will be hard to achieve but if these wrinkles appear after the age of forty your luck will change for the better (Fig 75).

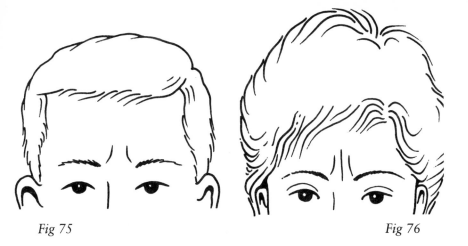

Fig 75   Fig 76

A third line running between these two lines reveals an anxious
and tense personality (Fig 76).

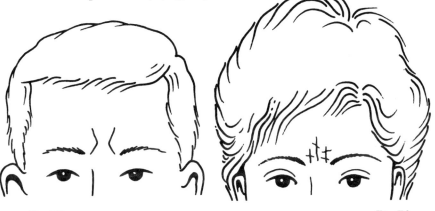

Fig 77   Fig 78

If the lines in the area of the yin t'ang slope outwards at an
angle you are likely to marry or establish a career late in life.
You will need to be determined and patient because it often
seems that circumstances conspire against you (Fig 77).

A set of crossing lines is an unlucky sign. It sometimes seems
that your life is a constant struggle and you cannot afford to
waste time or money (Fig 78). If the lines form deep wrinkles
you have difficulty controlling your temper.

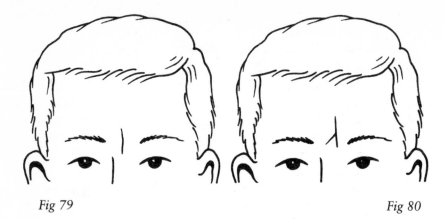

Fig 79   *Fig 80*

A single line running through the middle of the yin t'ang is called a hanging-needle and indicates anxiety and financial troubles (Fig 79). If another line branches out from the hanging-needle line your reading is improved. Someone in an influential position is likely to support you (Fig 80).

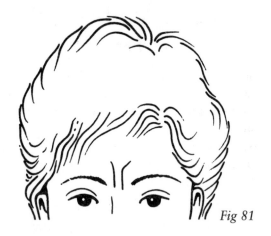

Fig 81

If one of the two lines in the yan t'ing curves towards the eyebrow at its upper point you may have embarrassed your family through a careless act, however, the upset will be remedied and your fortune will improve (Fig 81).

6. Shan Ken

The Heavenly and Human areas of the face meet at this point and it is also the meeting place of the yin side of your face (the right) and the yang side of your face (the left). The area should be slightly curved to establish a smooth contact point between Heaven and Earth and a balance between yin and yang. If a dark patch appears on this area, take care because you may suffer from a short period of illness. The darker the colour, the more serious the illness.

A mole on the shan ken denotes a journey away from home to find employment. A mole to one side of this area is a sign of stomach disorders.

7. Nien Shang

A mole in this area is a sign of turbulent romantic or family relationships. A mole in this area is also an indication of stomach disorders even if your health is generally strong.

8. Shou Shang

A protruding or lumpy bone in this area is a sign of an unsuccessful business venture at some time in your life. A mole or dirty mark on the shou shang forecasts an unsettled romance. If the skin on both sides of the shou shang is bright, clear and smooth you are likely to have a good dress sense and a strong stomach for eating and drinking.

9. Chun T'ou

If the skin is tinged black at the tip of the nose or if the tip is thin or sharp it will detract from your reading (see Chapter 8). Enlarged or black pores and hairs growing on the tip of the nose signify a period of hardship. It may be hard to earn a basic income or to balance family and working life.

10. Jen Chung

Readings are taken from the jen chung in relation to children. The ideal shape is narrow at the top near the nose and wider at the bottom near the lips and the lines should not be too deep or too flat. This is the sign of a happy, stable and prosperous family.

If the jen chung is wide at its upper point, narrow at its lower point and appears to be shallow you are unlikely to have many children. You also find it hard to trust others and to form friendships (Fig 82).

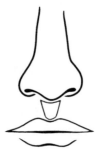 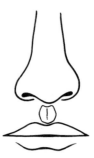

Fig 82   *Fig 83*

A straight line running through the jen chung denotes children late in life. A jen chung which is narrow at its upper and lower points but wide in the middle indicates intermittent family problems after middle age (Fig 83).

The jen chung is also meant to reveal the sex of your offspring. Narrow at its upper point and wide at its lower with distinct lines indicates more sons than daughters. Indistinct lines and a deep jen chung denotes more daughters than sons. The shape and lines of the jen chung become clearer with age so accurate readings cannot be made for children.

11. Shui Hsing

The area of the lips should be clear of blemishes, moist and bright in colour. They can reveal your character and attitude towards family, friends, work and romance. The variety of shapes is described in Chapter 7.

12. Ch'eng Chiang

It is believed that the ch'eng chiang rules water and therefore this area controls drinking and travelling by sea. If a dark patch appears, particularly in the morning, be careful what you drink and postpone any sea journeys until the dark patch has disappeared. White, green or dark red skin patches are a sign of stomach upset when you are eating or drinking.

13. Ti Ko

If the ti ko is slightly upturned, round and strong in appearance it is a sign of a healthy old age. A sharp, thin ti ko denotes a long life but there may be financial upsets or troubled friendships. If the nose and eyes are not well proportioned and the ti ko slopes to the right or the left you are easily offended and do not forget personal insults. You may know many people but you do not have many close friends. If this area is marked or scarred you have to rely on your own wits and skill to find an income since your family will not be able to support you. Dirty or smoky marks in this area are a sign of an accident or illness in your family.

THE TWELVE PALACES

The Twelve Palaces are in a variety of positions around the face. Some occur in two places, e.g. above each eyebrow, at each temple, above each eye and under each eye (see Fig 84 overleaf).

1. The Career Palace – Kuan Lu Kung

The Career palace is in the centre of the forehead. The area should not be too dome-shaped or sunken. An uneven forehead signifies difficult times ahead and you may have to work harder than imagined to achieve your goals. A mole on the forehead

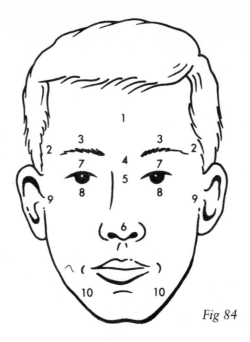

Fig 84

also denotes unexpected difficulties so patience and perseverance are needed. If your Career palace is even, clear and smooth
you are likely to form strong and long-lasting friendships.
When you are confronted by problems an influential friend is
likely to come to your help.

2. The Movement Palace – Ch'ien I Kung

The area around the temples should be slightly hollow but the
bones should not protrude. It indicates a long journey and safe
arrival but it is also a sign of business success. A sunken
Movement palace and a dull complexion can be read as
a warning not to undertake long journeys. A mole in the area
of the temples is a sign that you should not move too far
from home since there is the possibility of accident or loss of
possessions.

3. The Brothers' Palace – Hsiung Ti Kung

This palace refers to two types of brothers, those linked by blood and those linked by friendship. Long eyebrows denote a large family and short, distinct eyebrows indicate stable and happy family relationships. If the line of the eyebrow is broken near the middle you are likely to have an argumentative relationship with one of your brothers or sisters. Long, unruly hairs at the end of a long eyebrow are also an indication of a close but argumentative relationship with your family.

4. Life Palace – Min Kung

It is said that the Life palace is a mirror of the heart and of our emotions. If the area is wrinkled you are troubled and thoughtful but if the area is smooth and clear you have a fortunate life. An unbroken line running through the Life palace is a sign of an unexpected accident.

If the eyebrows are spaced widely apart you have plenty of ideas but often waste your time on projects that are unlikely to succeed. This wide gap can also denote a careless handling of your finances. By the age of thirty it is normal to have wrinkles in this area and an absence of them is a sign of a daydreamer or someone who does not pay serious attention to their work.

5. Sickness Palace – Chi O Kung

The condition of this area indicates the state of your health. A wrinkle-free and well-rounded Sickness palace is a sign of an honest, upright character and sturdy health. But if the area is crossed with irregular lines or marked by a mole you are likely to be indecisive and prone to minor illness. The Sickness palace is meant to give accurate readings at the ages of twenty-six, thirty and forty-one.

6.   Wealth Palace – Ts'ai Pai Kung

This palace indicates your ability in making or handling money. If the nose is prominent due to the fact that the cheeks and the sides of the nose are flat, you will have difficulty making money and holding on to it. The Chinese say that a nose without support is a 'lonesome hill'. If the nose is given strong support by the cheeks it is a sign that your career will involve buying and selling. A mole which can be seen looking at the nose straight signifies good luck. Natural marks or blemishes in this area are a sign that you take responsibility for your own problems but a scar is a warning to take care of your health and handle your relationships carefully around the age of forty-four.

7.   House and Farm Palace – T'ien Chai Kung

This palace sheds light on the success and happiness of your home life and career. Ideally the complexion should be clear and free of blemishes but if it is grey, smoky or scarred you may have trouble settling down at work or achieving peace of mind. You must give yourself time to think before you act. A mole or dark marks on the House and Farm palace is an indication that you do not pay much attention to the condition of your clothes or surroundings. A high eyebrow will improve this reading.

8.   Man and Woman Palace – Nan Nu Kung

If the area under the eyes is smooth and unblemished you are likely to have a large family and strong emotional bonds with your parents or children. This reading does allow for wrinkles. If the Man and Woman palace is lumpy, baggy or grey your family may be a continual source of concern. If the lines in this area cross each other you may leave home at an early age and are unlikely to maintain regular contact with your family.

Prominent veins and dark skin colouring are a sign of too many late nights or difficulty with your sleeping pattern.

9. Wife and Mistress Palace – Ch'i Ch'ien Kung

Readings are usually taken in this area to forecast the state of your romantic relationships. If your skin is soft and clear and the cheekbones do not protrude, your partner is likely to be a good judge of character and a reliable friend. Taut skin and thin muscles in this area are an indication that your marriage or relationship is passing through a difficult period.

A man's reading is usually taken from the left-hand side of his face and a woman's from the right-hand side. If a man or woman's skin is dented and the skin taut they cannot be trusted in their romantic life. It is difficult to obtain an accurate reading in this area if the individual is underweight or overweight. An additional reading can be taken from the eye. Interwoven fish-tail lines (the lines which form at the outside edge of the eye) are a sign of a quarrelsome relationship between husband and wife. A mole in this area is a sign of a flirtatious nature.

10. Servant's Palace – Nu P'u Kung

Readings are taken from this area to assess the quality of your friendships. If the palace has a well-rounded and discernible shape you are likely to have many trustworthy friends who trust your judgement. If the bone protrudes and the area is thin or lacks muscle tone you often upset others who have helped you with careless comments or actions.

11. Fortune and Virtue Palace – Fu Te Kung

There is no specific area associated with this palace. A reading is taken based on facial expressions since they often reflect your emotional state or personality.

12. Face Palace – Hsiang Mao Kung

You can take this reading by examining the balance of the facial features. A dull complexion or dents in the skin detract from a positive reading.

THE TWELVE EARTHLY BRANCHES

The Twelve Earthly Branches are used to forecast the condition of your health and emotional state from the age of seventy to one hundred. They are traditional terms used in Chinese astrology and are also associated with the twelve Chinese animal years and the Jade Emperor, the ruler of Heaven. The Twelve Earthly Branches appear around the edge of the face in a clockwise direction (Fig 85). There are no specific readings in relation to each area and in order to take a reading you have to take into account the condition and colour of the skin. Even if the skin is wrinkled it should still be clear and evenly coloured.

THE FIVE MOUNTAINS

The Five Mountains are associated with different parts of the face (Fig 86):

1. CHIN   North Mountain
2. FOREHEAD   South Mountain
3. LEFT CHEEK   East Mountain
4. RIGHT CHEEK West Mountain
5. NOSE   Central Mountain

The Central mountain, the nose, is said to be the 'commander' of the face. If one of the other mountains of the face is hollow,

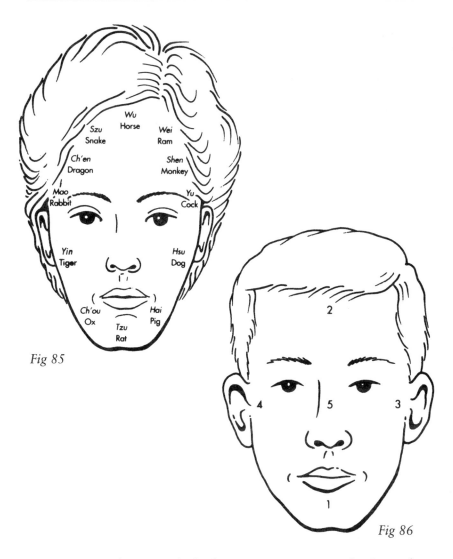

Fig 85

Fig 86

uneven or weak, particularly the East or West ones, the Central mountain lacks support. This is a warning that you cannot rely on others in a crisis so it is necessary to maintain a strong, independent spirit.

It is said that a woman whose forehead is smooth, well-rounded and large in relation to the rest of the face will marry several times. A traditional forecast predicts seven marriages.

THE FOUR RIVERS

The Four Rivers are associated with the following areas:

EARS	Kong River
EYES	Ho River
MOUTH	Wai River
NOSE	Chai River

According to traditional physiognomy, the waters of these rivers should be clear and clean. This implies that these features should ideally be clear of phlegm or infections so that your senses are sharp. The area between the bottom of the nose and the top of the upper lip is known as the yan chung and is believed to be the channel that connects the Four Rivers.

If the upper part of the yan chung is wider than the lower part or is slightly bent, the flow of the river is hindered. As well as influencing the flow of the Four Rivers, the yan chung is linked to family happiness.

MOLES

Red or black moles are considered lucky but grey or light black moles are less fortunate. The readings given below are for moles that appear in one or more of the nineteen positions listed **A** – **S** in Fig 87.

A – an argumentative relationship with your parents

B and **C** – you do not listen to advice from your family

D – a sign of impatience

E – a gullible nature and lack of attention to detail

F – do not take too many physical risks

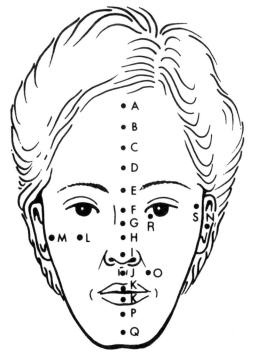

Fig 87

G and **H** – take care of your health; do not ignore warning signs

I – handle money carefully and avoid gambling

J – be careful not to become preoccupied with money; relax and enjoy yourself

K – a healthy appetite for food and life

L – it may be hard to achieve your career ambitions

M – be extra careful when you are near fire

N – a sign of an obedient and respectful nature

O – pay attention to your health between the ages of fifty-six and fifty-seven

P – pay attention to your health around the age of fifty-four

Q – a sign of an unsettled childhood; your family may not be able to support you financially when you need help.

R – if the mole is close to the eyelid you enjoy the company of the opposite sex and if the mole is underneath the eye the demands of your working life make it difficult to spend as much time with your family as you would like

S – a sign of an active romantic life

Reading the Five Features

The Five Features of Chinese physiognomy are the eyes, eyebrows, mouth, nose and ears. If one of the features is not in harmony with the others, for example a bent nose or a damaged lip, this will detract from your overall reading. Conversely, if four of the features are discordant but the fifth has an ideal colour and shape your reading will improve. This is likened to pouring a cup of clean water into murky water to improve its visibility.

The face should not be examined in isolation from other parts of the body. All areas should be taken into account in order for an accurate prediction to be made.

5

THE EYES

THE EYES are the most important feature on the face since they are believed to control the other four features. Bright, clear and alert eyes will improve the quality of the overall facial reading. The descriptions of the eye shapes do not mention the colour since the art of physiognomy originally applied to the Chinese people whose eyes are usually brown. The character of the eye is now interpreted according to the shape and clarity of the eye itself. The eye shapes which are included in this section are relevant to any race.

While the other features on the face alter over the years, the eye remains a constant feature. Ideally the iris should fill a large space in the eye and the colour should be distinct. The eye should not be bloodshot, the pupil should be clear and bright, and the eye itself should not protrude or look angry.

POINTS TO LOOK FOR:

- The reading for the eyes is marred by a dull pupil or very low eyebrows which are compared to clouds obscuring the moon. This is a sign of someone who is full of plans but rarely puts them into effect.

- Large, wide-open eyes are an indication of an easy-going, friendly nature and a good head for business.

- If there is a dark, shadowy tinge to the eye it is a sign of an active intellect and a creative nature.

- Dull, protruding eyes or round, staring eyes are an indication that you are willing to work but events rarely turn out as successfully as you had hoped.

- A constant gaze denotes an honest, reliable character who is attentive to the opinions of others and open to negotiation.

- If the eyes rise upwards while speaking it is a sign of confidence. You are not afraid to speak your mind and are sure of your beliefs.

- If the face remains level but the eyes dart from left to right while you are speaking your head is full of ideas, plans and schemes.

- If the eyes are slowly wandering around while you are speaking you plan carefully and probably have a good business sense but you are not always reliable.

- If there is no fold on your eyelid you are likely to react strongly to emotional situations.

- If you are above forty years of age and have many lines (fishtails or crow's feet) at the outside corner you are a good organiser and enjoy the challenge of sorting out difficult situations.

- Fishtail wrinkles or crow's feet that are shaped like scissors so that one runs upwards and the other crosses it downwards are a sign that you find it hard to accept advice from others, particularly your family.

- Eyes which are bright and well shaped but watery are an indication of a healthy sexual appetite.

- If the white of the eye covers a large area but the iris is small you are likely to be accident prone. Although you try hard to avoid trouble, sometimes it seems to come your way.

TYPES OF EYES

Triangular Eyes

The white of the eyes and iris have distinct colours and the eyes are alert. This eye usually appears with a strong eyebrow (Fig 88).

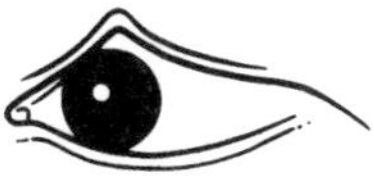

Fig 88

This combination is believed to be a sign of success, wealth and prosperity. You have a competitive nature and a determined outlook. You observe what is happening around you and think your plans through before you decide on a plan of action. In your desire to succeed you are likely to offend those around you.

Wheel Eyes

These eyes have coloured lines in the iris and are known as angry eyes (Fig 89).

Fig 89

You have a physical and forthright nature that can be over-powering at times. Your need to express what you feel could cause ill feeling amongst your friends or family.

Fire Wheel Eyes

The edge of the iris has a light green, red or blue ring. Sometimes there is a lighter coloured ring at the centre of the eye (Fig 90).

Fig 90

You are quickly moved to anger if someone or something upsets you. You have an alert nature which enables you to spot strengths as well as weaknesses and if you are not pleased with what you see you will soon comment on it.

Sand Eyes

There are flecks of colour in the iris and the eyes have a sharp, alert look (Fig 91).

Fig 91

You enjoy discussion and quickly pick up on points that other people make. You are never short of an answer and are quick to spot a weakness in someone else's conversation which can make you appear quarrelsome and unsettled.

Mole Eyes

There is a fleck of colour in the white of the eye (Fig 92).

Fig 92

You seem to pass through unlucky periods when nothing works out in the way you planned. You enjoy life's luxuries and are tempted to spend money as soon as you receive it.

Drunk Eyes

The eyes are bloodshot and have a sleepy look. The iris slopes downwards, the whites of the eyes have a yellow tinge and the fishtail has many short wrinkles (Fig 93).

Fig 93

You enjoy the company of the opposite sex and have a lively sexual appetite. You are also likely to pass through unlucky periods when nothing seems to go right. All you can do is be patient and wait for these disruptions to pass.

Unwrinkled Eyes

The eye has few wrinkles even in middle and old age. The tail of the eye is rounded (Fig 94).

Fig 94

The shape of this eye is a sign of intelligence. You have strong powers of persuasion and can be very convincing even in the face of opposition. This ability to persuade others to follow your lead could cause trouble in your romantic life.

Pea Blossom Eyes

The eyes are long and bow-shaped. The iris and the white are cloudy (Fig 95).

Fig 95

You tend to observe others cautiously instead of looking straight at them while you assess situations. You have creative talent and are likely to be successful in the arts. You also enjoy a lively social life and romantic involvement.

Elephant Eyes

There are wrinkles above and below the eye. The eye itself is narrow and long (Fig 96).

Fig 96

You are popular amongst friends and colleagues and are well liked for your sympathetic nature. If someone is in trouble you will usually put yourself out to help them. You also have a creative nature and approach your work with sensitivity and enthusiasm.

Lion Eyes

The eyes are large and the iris and the whites are clear. The iris is set at the top of the eye and there are several lines on the lid (Fig 97).

Fig 97

You take your career seriously and are capable of achieving a responsible position. You are respected for your judgement of people and situations.

Tiger Eyes

The iris is golden coloured and the gaze is straight and steady. There are no lines underneath the eye but there is a line on the eyelid. The fishtails are short and scattered (Fig 98).

Fig 98

Your attitude and behaviour inspire others to behave sensibly. People usually listen to you and take notice of your suggestions and questions. There are times when you prefer your own company and there are times when you have no choice but to work or live alone.

Crane Eyes

The eyes are large and the iris is round, clear and centrally placed in the eye. The eyes are long and there are usually two or more wrinkles on the eyelid (Fig 99).

Fig 99

You have an honest and forthright nature. Your natural attitude towards life and your innate concern for others enable you not only to make friends easily but also to keep them.

Egret Eyes

These are long in shape with slight yellow tinges in the iris or in the white of the eye. The iris is sometimes positioned high in the eye and there is a long wrinkle in the eyelid. There are usually no long wrinkles under the eye (Fig 100).

Fig 100

You often choose to work alone or live alone, to live life at your own pace or on your own terms. Although you are close to family and friends you do not automatically turn to them when you need help.

Wild Goose Eyes

The pupils are large and there is a golden tinge to the iris. There is a definite wrinkle above and below the eye. The eye has a long and well-defined shape (Fig 101).

Fig 101

You take a relaxed outlook on life and have a lively and out-going nature. It is unlikely that you will ever be short of friends. Although the chance for wealth or promotion may come your way you are not an ambitious person and are content with an average job and status.

Swallow Eyes

The eyes are deep set with a long line above and below. The eyes themselves are clear and bright (Fig 102).

Fig 102

You are a trustworthy friend and faithfully keep your promises. You will never be very wealthy but that is not your main concern since a comfortable lifestyle satisfies you.

Horse Eyes

The lower lid has several folds of skin and the upper lid is soft. The fishtail wrinkles at the outer corner of the eye grow downwards. The eye itself is slightly bulging and watery (Fig 103).

Fig 103

You have drive and energy although your efforts are not always rewarded as you might expect. In order to achieve what you want you may have to persevere regardless of the setbacks in your professional or private life.

Lamb Eyes

There is a dark cast to the eye and the iris has a yellow tinge; sometimes it is possible to spot wheel-shaped lines in the iris. The upper lid has a marked fold but the lower one does not. The skin beneath the eye is flat, thin and lined. The fishtail wrinkles on the outer corner of the eye are scattered (Fig 104).

Fig 104

You are a determined and successful worker but it seems that there is little time to enjoy the fruits of this work. Somehow

your plans for your free time are swallowed up by incidents beyond your control. There are times when you have to rely on your own initiative since support from colleagues or family does not always materialise or is not wanted.

Oxen Eyes

The colour of the iris and the white of the eyes are usually very clear. The eyes are large but do not protrude (Fig 105).

Fig 105

You have a relaxed, gentle nature and are unlikely to have emotional outbursts. If there are wrinkles above and below the eye and the fishtail wrinkles at the outside edge rise upwards you have a trustworthy character and will fulfil your promises.

Pig Eyes

The colour of the iris is dark and muddy and the skin on the lid is thick and heavy (Fig 106).

Fig 106

You are prone to losing your temper and often criticise or comment without considering your words beforehand. Instead of acting on impulse, try to relax and enjoy life around you.

Monkey Eyes

The iris is dark with a yellow tinge and positioned high in the eye. The eyes are short in length and the line above the eye is rounded and slopes steeply towards the eye corner and beyond (Fig 107).

Fig 107

You have a bright, outgoing and courageous nature which is respected by others. You are skilled at making plans and carrying them out and are likely to maintain an optimism even through difficult times. Like the monkey, you probably enjoy fruit.

POSITION OF THE IRIS

Top Three White

The iris is at the bottom of the eye and there is white on three sides (Fig 108).

Fig 108

You are determined and confident but there are times when you lose your temper too quickly. You are easily frustrated by the inability of others to understand an issue or to act quickly. You are honest with your opinions; so honest that you sometimes appear tactless or unintentionally cruel.

Bottom Three White

The iris is in the upper part of the eye and there are three areas of white, one on each side and one beneath the iris (Fig 109).

Fig 109

You have an astute nature and know what you want and how to achieve it although there are times when you act without considering the circumstances or people around you. Your determination to do things your way could cause disruption or disagreements with others.

Upward-growing Eyebrow Hairs

Upward-growing eyebrow hairs are again a sign of courage but also an indication of a hot temper (Fig 111). Your tendency to speak or act on the spur of the moment upsets others. There are times when you regret your hasty remarks.

 *Fig 111*

Downward-growing Eyebrow Hairs

Downward-growing hairs denote nervousness and lack of confidence (Fig 112). You try to avoid confrontation but there are also times when you try to avoid the consequences of your actions. If you are in a marriage or a partnership it may take a long time for the relationship to find a balance.

 *Fig 112*

Cuddling Hair

If the hairs at the top of the eyebrow grow downwards and those on the bottom grow upwards so that they meet in the middle, you worry, often unnecessarily, over routine matters (Fig 113). This type of eyebrow is known in Chinese physiognomy as 'cuddling hair'.

 *Fig 113*

Scattered Hair Growth

If the eyebrow is thick and dark and the hairs grow in different directions, you may have to deal with unexpected setbacks (Fig 114). These may be problems created by someone in a position of authority.

 *Fig 114*

Thin and Clear Eyebrows

Thin, clear eyebrows which are light in colour are the sign of a calm and untroubled nature (Fig 115). You like to avoid demanding work and when confronted by a problem you try to pass through it quickly and quietly.

 *Fig 115*

EYEBROW SHAPES

The readings that follow are related to specific shapes although not everybody can be matched to these types. You may have to mix and match to find your particular eyebrow shape. This section opens with three general eyebrow shapes that may help you if you cannot find a specific reading.

Long Eyebrow

The eyebrow grows beyond the eyetail. The hairs lie in the same direction and have a glossy appearance (Fig 116).

Fig 116

You have a good intellect and are a talented speaker and debater. You are likely to be on friendly terms with family, friends and colleagues. If this eyebrow is combined with well-balanced facial features, it is a sign that middle age is a lucky period in your life.

106

Short Eyebrow

The hairs on the eyebrow are rough and uneven in length. The eyebrow is shorter than the eye (Fig 117).

Fig 117

You are likely to come from a small family who try to keep in contact with one another but their relationships are strained by disagreements and arguments. It may take many years to find a career that suits your temperament.

Big Eyebrow

The eyebrow is wide, long and well formed (Fig 118).

Fig 118

You are not afraid to deal with dissent or difficult situations. You have a courageous nature and will speak out in support of others. You are likely to be the more dominant partner in a marriage or a relationship.

1 Character Eyebrow

Although the hairs are thick, the roots are strong and can be seen quite clearly. The eyebrow is straight, of medium length and round at the end. It should grow beyond the eye tail and looks like the Chinese character for the number 1 ▬ (Fig 119).

Fig 119

You are likely to come from a large family who maintain close links with one another. You will probably establish yourself successfully in a business career at an early age and will enjoy a good reputation at work. This eyebrow also denotes a long and stable marriage.

8 Character Eyebrow

The eyebrow is Y-shaped, the hair growth is thin and the hairs are scattered at the eyebrow tail. The shape of the eyebrow resembles the Chinese character 8 (Fig 120).

Fig 120

This is the eyebrow of a loner. You guard your privacy and find it difficult to relax or socialise with others. It may be hard to find a romantic partner who matches your temperament. You do not always make the most of career opportunities that come your way. You will, however, always be economically independent and will enjoy a long life.

Ghost Eyebrow

This eyebrow is low on the browbone, curved in shape and short in length. The hairs do not follow the flow of the curve but grow upwards and lie straight (Fig 121).

Fig 121

You find it hard to trust others and are suspicious of their motives. You rarely reveal your inner thoughts and worries and your attitude can appear sharp and antagonistic. It may take a while to find a suitable career or romantic partner with whom you feel comfortable and who understands you.

Sharp Knife Eyebrow

This is a dagger-shaped eyebrow; it has a sharp head and widens towards the tail. The hairs are thick and rough (Fig 122).

Fig 122

You have an astute nature and rarely miss the opportunity to make a profit or gain an advantage. When you are faced with a problem or embarrassing situation you usually find the easiest way out. You are confident and happy to tell others about your achievements or conquests.

Rolling, Circular Eyebrow

The hairs are dark and thick and curl in the same direction. This is an unusual eyebrow and frequently seen on the faces of powerful leaders, usually in the military (Fig 123).

Fig 123

Broom Eyebrow

The hairs on the head of the eyebrow are thick but widen out to become scattered and sparse towards the tail (Fig 124).

Fig 124

You are likely to come from a large family but do not maintain regular contact with them. Distance and financial and emotional difficulties prevent members of your family helping one another. If you have your own family it will take time and patience for you to build close relationships. Although you have enough money to survive, you are never likely to be wealthy.

Little Broom Eyebrow

This eyebrow is the same shape as the broom eyebrow but shorter; it does not reach the eyetail (Fig 125 overleaf).

 *Fig 125*

You can be impatient and lose your temper easily. You are also adept at spotting a good opportunity and finding your way out of trouble. Your family relationships are highly strung, and arguments or disagreements may be a regular feature of your domestic life.

Clear and Beautiful Eyebrow

This eyebrow is long and slightly curved. The hairs arch in the same direction and the roots cannot be seen clearly. If the eyebrow is short and high but still has the same hair growth, then the reading is the same (Fig 126).

 *Fig 126*

You are a trustworthy friend and business associate and can be relied upon to keep your promises. When disagreements do arise you put in extra effort to find a compromise and keep the peace. Your ability to judge others and treat them fairly is likely to bring you good fortune in your career and family life.

Mortal Eyebrow

The hairs on the eyebrow are long, rough and thick. Although the eyebrow is short, the body is bushy and wide and the eyebrow tail grows downwards (Fig 127).

 *Fig 127*

You find it hard to establish close relationships and are regarded as a loner. You enjoy the company of the opposite sex, and once you have come to know and trust someone you do form close friendships. You are likely to have children late in life and cannot rely on your parents, brothers or sisters to provide the support you may need.

Sword Eyebrow

The eyebrow grows high on the brow and is straight, long, wide and almost flat. The hairs grow in the same direction and the body of the eyebrow is thicker at its end (Fig 128).

 *Fig 128*

You are astute and a good judge of character. You are a born leader and have the ability and the wisdom to run a successful business or organisation. When you are confronted by problems you have the wisdom and the strength to resolve them peacefully. This eyebrow denotes a long life and a large family.

Rising Eyebrow

The eyebrow is long, rising evenly beyond the tail, rising like a long knife (Fig 129).

 *Fig 129*

You are determined and find it hard to admit defeat. Your need to have everything planned the way you want can make you appear dominant or argumentative. You like to win at work or at play, and you frequently do come first. You will be successful at an early age and you will continue to be moderately successful as you grow older. As a result of your determination, your family relationships may suffer.

Willow Leaf Eyebrow

The eyebrow hairs become easily tangled and their roots can be seen. The eyebrow is long and has a slightly curved shape (Fig 130 overleaf).

111

Fig 130

You have an open, friendly and honest character which makes you a popular friend. You also have a lively mind and a good aptitude for learning. You enjoy friendships and relationships with the opposite sex and provide good company. Your intellect and personality give you the potential to be wealthy and at some point you may be helped by an influential friend. You may not start a family until late in life.

New Moon Eyebrow

The eyebrow is long, well formed and high above the eye. The hairs are glossy and grow in the same direction (Fig 131).

Fig 131

You are a thoughtful and honest person and are well respected by those who know you at work and socially. You are likely to come from a large family with whom you maintain close contact. You will probably be a trustworthy and devoted partner and parent.

Burial or Crying Eyebrow

The eyebrow head is higher than the tail and the hairs grow downwards, scattering in different directions. The eyebrow does not grow beyond the tail (Fig 132).

Fig 132

It is hard to tell what you are thinking; the way you speak and act often hides your real feelings. You are very astute and make the most of opportunities that come your way. Your quick-witted nature will enable you to succeed in business dealings although you may offend others in the process.

Long Life Eyebrow

The body of the eyebrow is wide and the hairs are longer at the eyebrow tail than at the eyebrow head. They are dark in colour and have a glossy sheen. The eyebrow head curves slightly downwards (Fig 133).

Fig 133

You will have a long and successful life. You are suited to a creative career, particularly as a writer, and may find fame and wealth in this field. You have a friendly and kind disposition and are a popular companion, especially with the opposite sex.

Dragon Eyebrow

The eyebrow rises in a straight line and then slopes down past the eyetail. The hairs are bright and glossy and the eyebrow generally has a good appearance (Fig 134).

Fig 134

This shape eyebrow is an indication that you come from a large family. You are clever, interested in the world around you and have a good head for business. You are not afraid to speak your mind or to take a prominent role in difficult situations. You are likely to be wealthy and respected by your colleagues and family.

Silkworm Eyebrow

The body of the eyebrow is curled and the eyebrow rises upwards. It has a smooth, even shape and the hairs have a glossy sheen (Fig 135).

Fig 135

You are clever, intelligent and trusted by friends and colleagues. You are suited to office work or a career in a disciplined field. During your life opportunities will appear that could bring you wealth and fame.

Lion-shaped Eyebrow

The eyebrow curls along its length and the body is wide and curved. Although the eyebrow is thick the roots are still visible. The shape resembles a lion lying down (Fig 136).

Fig 136

This eyebrow can give you an angry appearance but this belies your thoughtful nature. You are suited to concentrated, regular routines. Your generous nature will win the respect of colleagues and friends although there may be recurrent domestic quarrels. This eyebrow also denotes long life.

THE LIPS

YOUR MOUTH is a good indicator of your character. Its shape and size denote kindness or severity, happiness or depression, selfishness or generosity.

A good mouth is well proportioned with slightly upturned corners. The corners are known as ling or sea corners (Fig 137).

Fig 137

The lips should be full in relation to the size of the face, and red in colour. A reading for the mouth will depend on its balance with other facial features and the overall size of the face. In Chinese physiognomy it is luckier to have a large mouth combined with a small face than the other way round.

POINTS TO LOOK FOR:

- A large mouth with weak sea corners or uneven lips is a sign of a sharp tongue and a hasty manner. Your tendency to jump into action without careful forethought could result in financial loss.

- Lips which purse together when the mouth is naturally closed are an indication of a cross and worried nature. You try too hard to please others, particularly those in authority.

- Full, large, bright and well-balanced lips are considered to be the sign of a healthy body and strong stomach. You enjoy life and all it has to offer.

- A bow-shaped mouth which looks as though it is in a permanent smile denotes creativity and culture. You are more interested in theatre, film or art than you are in material possessions. You find it easy to form close, sensitive friendships (Fig 138).

- A large, wide mouth and a strongly built body signify determination. You make the most of opportunities and aim to achieve, regardless of any difficulties in your way. You are not always successful but that does not deter you. You are likely to lead a busy life that leaves little time for reflection.

- If the bottom part of the upper lip covers the lower lip in the centre of the mouth you are confident and determined, persuading others to follow your ideas or decisions (Fig 139).

- If the upper lip is thin and lower lip thick you have an astute nature and quickly get out of difficult situations (Fig 140).

- Thin lips are a sign of unhappiness or bitterness. It may be hard for you to find stability and contentment in your life.

- Thick well-balanced upper and lower lips are an indication of a steady, honest nature. Your attitude towards life is positive and this is conveyed through your relationships and your work.

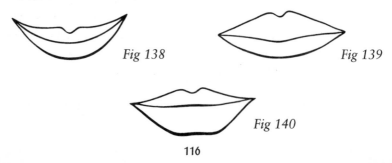

Fig 138   Fig 139

Fig 140

Fish Mouth

The mouth is wide, the lips are thin and the sea corners slope downwards to a point (Fig 146).

Fig 146

Finding a suitable career and maintaining it may be one of the hardest tasks you will have to face. There may be useful financial support from your family but this will not immediately resolve all your problems.

Lotus Leaf Mouth

The lips are thin and dull in colour. The mouth is long and the sea corners slope downwards slightly (Fig 147).

Fig 147

You find it uncomfortable to talk about your own weaknesses or faults and may even find it hard to admit them to yourself. It is difficult for you to face criticism and you are happier discussing the lives and affairs of others.

Unbalanced Mouth

One side of the mouth slopes down and the other up so the mouth is lopsided (Fig 148).

Fig 148

You enjoy conversation and are interested in the events around you but you are prone to exaggeration when you are describing what you or others have done. The Chinese say that you 'speak through a magnifying glass'. There are lucky periods in your life when you may receive unexpected financial help but you are likely to spend it as quickly as you received it. You are easily hurt in your emotional relationships.

Cherry Mouth

The face is an average size and the corners of the mouth slope upwards. The lips are red and bright and the teeth are small. These teeth are traditionally described as 'pomegranate teeth' since they are close together and have a clear, crystal appearance (Fig 149).

Fig 149

You are intelligent and wise. It is not unusual for others to come to you for advice or help. You also have a generous nature and are sensitive to the needs of others. If you are ever in trouble someone in a position of influence is likely to help you out.

THE TONGUE

The ideal tongue is large and wide and moves in a lively way when you speak. A short, sleepy tongue is considered to be unlucky. If you can lick the tip of your nose it is a sign of prosperity and good fortune. A long, narrow tongue or a short, rough tongue is an indication of unexpected setbacks and disappointments in your life. With patience and effort you will overcome these obstacles.

The ideal tongue should be deep red since this traditionally signifies respectability and financial success. A tongue with wrinkles running down the length is a sign of honesty, but wrinkles running across the tongue are an indication of a short temper and outspoken nature. Criss-crossing lines on the tongue refer to career or financial success.

- If your fa ling spread out in a wide arc from the nose and beyond the mouth you are likely to be successful and well known, particularly in a creative, commercial or administrative field (Fig 156).

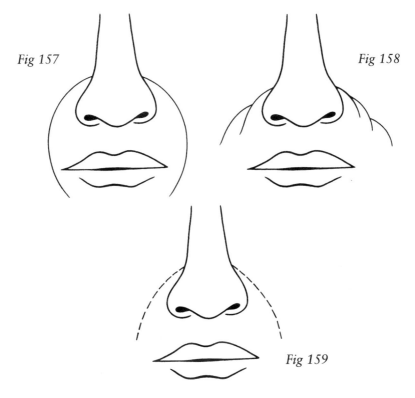

Fig 157

Fig 158

Fig 159

- Fa ling which curve inwards to lock below the corners of the mouth denote a long and healthy life (Fig 157).

- Fa ling which branch in several places indicate the possibility of domestic or career upheavals. You may have to leave a familiar place in order to improve your situation (Fig 158).

- When the fa ling are missing, faint or broken there will be lucky periods throughout your life which arrive just in time to help you out of problems. There will also be times when you regret or reconsider your career due to lack of job satisfaction (Fig 159).

THE NOSE

IN ORDER to give an accurate reading for the nose you also have to consider the shape of the cheekbones. It is said that the nose is like an emperor and the cheekbones are the guards on either side. The nose is also traditionally said to be a mountain which is set in the middle of four other mountains. The left cheek is the eastern mountain, the right cheek is the western mountain, the forehead is the southern mountain and the chin is the northern mountain. (Chinese maps traditionally place south at the top; see page 16.) The nose is the most important feature and controls the other four. Since the cheekbones are said to be the guards of the face, they should lean towards the nose. If they are hollow or flat the nose has no support.

As with other areas of physiognomy, the combined features should be well balanced since a weakness in one area detracts from the overall reading. The ideal cheekbones should be rounded but not obvious. High cheek bones are luckier than low ones (Fig 160 shows the classic position for a cheekbone).

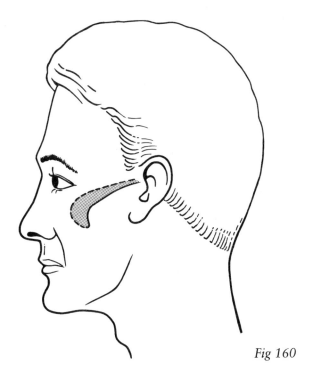

Fig 160

POINTS TO LOOK FOR:

- If the left cheekbone is higher than the right, the nose is not in control. It is a sign that you are cautious of carrying out a bold venture or taking risks.

- If the cheekbones are well formed but the nose is flat or weak, you are easily persuaded to act or think in a certain way.

- If the line of the cheekbone protrudes and the skin is taut, you may find that you just miss out on lucky opportunities. It sometimes seems that you are in the wrong place at the wrong time. You are likely to spend money as soon as you receive it and, when you can, you enjoy living the good life.

- Cheekbones that are flat or slightly dented are an indication of a retiring nature. You do not want to be given unnecessary responsibilities and you are not driven by ambition.

NOSE SHAPES

The nose should not be too thin nor should it be too upturned. If you look at someone straight on, you should not be able to see the nostrils too clearly. You can usually tell by looking straight at a nose whether it is strongly built and if the air passageways are clear. The skin on the nose should be bright and clear and the tip of the nose should be rounded and muscular.

According to Chinese physiognomy the nose is divided into six areas (Fig 161). The left nostril is called lan t'ai and the right is known as t'ing wei. Together they are referred to as lan t'ing. The nose is further divided into four more areas: the shan ken, the nien shang, the shou shang and the chun t'ou. The shan ken is at the top, the nien shang and the shou shang are in the middle, and the chun t'ou is the tip. If the nien shang and the shou shang are rounded, and the other features are in harmony, a prosperous life is forecast. The nien shang and the shou shang combined are called nien shou.

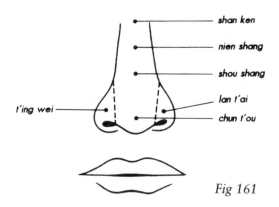

Fig 161

A long nose is considered more desirable than a short one but the proportions of the nose should always be examined in relation to the rest of the face.

- If the nostrils are clearly visible and have oval-shaped holes you have a good control over your money. You find it equally easy to save or spend money. You dislike risks and usually have finances to fall back on in times of emergency.

- Well-shaped rounded nostrils signify a decisive, orderly nature. You are a perfectionist; not only is your own life in order but you like to organise the people around you also.

- If your nose has a grey tinge to the skin you are full of plans and ideas. Even in the face of apparently insurmountable problems you continue to search for a solution.

Sword Nose

The nose is large and high on the face. The bridge of the nose is sharp and hard to the touch (Fig 168).

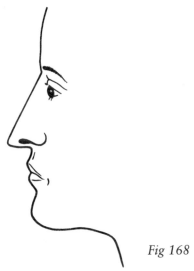

Fig 168

You have an unsteady and sometimes tempestuous relationship with your family. Sometimes the arguments are forgotten quickly, but others take longer to heal. It takes you time and effort to feel comfortable in new situations, which may make you appear withdrawn or unfriendly.

Lonely Mountain Nose

The end of the nose is very high. The nien shou (two middle portions of the nose combined) are flat and the cheekbones are usually very flat (Fig 169).

You like to experience life and make the most of opportunities. You are not always as successful as you would like to be but most of the time you are content with your career and domestic life. You will have to learn to be self-reliant since friends and family are not always able to support or help you when you need them.

Hairy Nose

The nostrils are large and hairy. The bridge of the nose is strong but the tip of the nose is thin and flat (Fig 170).

You have a strong competitive streak. If you have a good disposable income or if you suddenly win money you are tempted to spend it immediately. There will be difficult times in your life but you are courageous and where others fail you try to succeed. You may be successful in many areas but you cannot always hold on to this success.

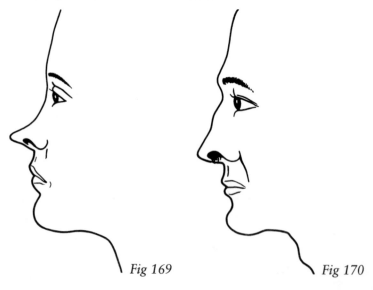

Fig 169   *Fig 170*

Bun-bridge Nose

The nien shou (the middle position of the nose) protrudes and even though the nose looks large at first glance, it is thin and lacks muscle (Fig 171).

You are a humorous and honest person but your behaviour is erratic. Your unpredictability sometimes affects your friendships. Your work has more than its fair share of highs and lows but you have the energy to work through these challenges.

Three-bends Nose

The shan ken is dented and the nien shou protrudes. The tip of the nose is sharp and thin (Fig 172).

Just when everything seems to be running well problems crop up for you, but with time you will learn to manage these setbacks. Life is never likely to be predictable or boring for you.

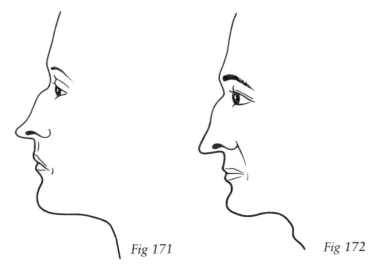

Fig 171　　　　　　　　　　　*Fig 172*

Collapsed Nose

The nose is soft and weak, the tip of the nose is small and the bridge is flat. The bridge of the nose appears to sink inwards and the nostrils can be seen clearly if you look directly at the face (Fig 173 overleaf).

You are astute and a good opportunist. If you identify a chance for making a profit you are likely to grab it although events don't always work out as you planned. There are times when you don't earn as much as you estimated. You try to avoid trouble and taking on unnecessary responsibilities.

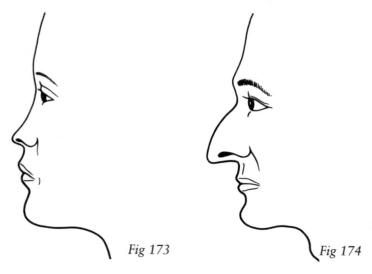

Fig 173

Fig 174

Eagle Beak Nose

The nose is thin and the nien shou protrudes. The tip of the nose is sharp and hooked (Fig 174).

You like to pursue your own interests and enjoy the challenge of making money or becoming well known in the process. You sometimes forget that others may not share your interests or your enthusiasm. Good opportunities do appear intermittently but do not last for a long time.

Knot Nose

The nose has a rounded lump on the nien shou which has the appearance of a knot (Fig 175).

You are strong willed and find it hard to accept advice. If you are faced with unexpected problems you are likely to abandon what you are doing if you do not agree with others. You do, however, have a generous heart and approach your work energetically. You will never be wealthy but you will have a circle of firm friends and colleagues.

Protruding Nostril Nose

The nose is large and the tip is rounded and slightly upturned. If you look straight on it is almost possible to see the complete nostril (Fig 176).

You have an easy-going attitude to money. If it is there you spend it freely and happily and if there is no money you go without. You don't complain about poverty and others share in your extravagance when you are prosperous.

Unbalanced Nose

One side of the nose is lower than the other. The reading for this nose improves if the tip of the nose is rounded and the bridge is straight (Fig 177).

If you do not have the additional features mentioned above you will find it hard to invest wisely or keep control of capital. During upheavals or disappointments in your middle age you may have to rely on your own initiative to survive.

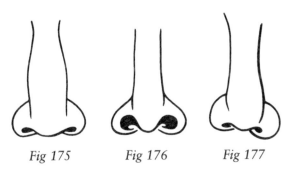

Fig 175   *Fig 176*   *Fig 177*

Sage's Son Nose

The top of the nose is wide and straight and the line of the nose is well formed and strong. The main body of the nose is long and continues in a straight line to the forehead. The nostrils are well balanced and the skin is clear (Fig 178).

You enjoy life and all it has to offer. You have a positive and egalitarian attitude; you treat everyone with equal respect. You also have a strong sense of justice and are not afraid to stand up and defend your beliefs.

Lamb Nose

The tip of the nose is bulbous and both nostrils are easily distinguished. The top of the nose is strong and the main body of the nose is rounded (Fig 179).

You are likely to be hard-working and successful in your profession. You do not like others to obstruct you and you can be resentful or unthoughtful if you do not get your own way. You are, however, respected for your determination and energy.

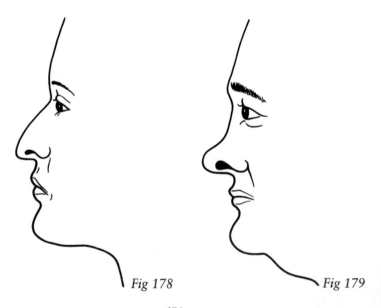

Fig 178

Fig 179

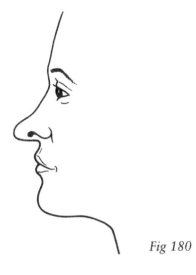

Fig 180

Deer Nose

The tip of the nose is round and the main body of the nose is slightly indented but the nose still has the appearance of being strong and well formed (Fig 180).

You have a kind nature and can be relied on to help others or to keep your promises. You are faithful to colleagues or friends even if you have only known them for a short time. The Deer nose is an indication of a long life and a large family.

THE EARS

THERE is a saying in Chinese physiognomy that since the ear is the only feature that does not move, it cannot lie. The ears are equally as important when taking a reading as the other features of the face.

The outline of the ear is called the 'wheel' and it is divided into three parts. The top part is called the Heaven wheel, the middle part is called the Human wheel and the bottom part is called the Earth wheel. The inner ridge of the ear is referred to as the inner ring. The ear pearl is the bottom, fleshy part of the ear and the centre of the ear is the ear hole (Fig 181).

The ideal ear should grow close to the head and be set on a level between the eyebrow and the tip of the nose. The ear should feel slightly fleshy and the wheel and the inner ring should be an even, smooth shape. This is known as the 'five fortune ear'. The five fortunes are luck, long life, good fortune, a peaceful home and a happy family. A reading for the ear is weakened by an indistinct ear line or wheel and patchy skin colouring.

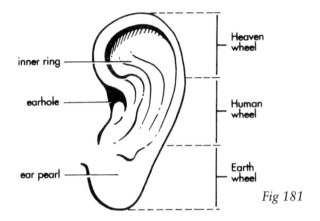

Fig 181

POINTS TO LOOK FOR:

- A small ear combined with a grey tinge to the skin is sign that you find it hard to keep a secret. You like to talk to others and let them know the latest news or information.

- If the top of the ear is at a higher level than the eyebrow and the ear pearl at a higher level than the tip of the nose it is a sign of intelligence. You are also an exhibitionist and like to attract attention by your dress, actions or words. You are a capable worker but your style of working doesn't always appeal to your employers.

- If the lower part of your ear is on a level with the tip of your nose, you are determined and successful, particularly in creative fields.

- A soft, fleshy ear set at a lower level than the eyebrow but reaching the same level as the tip of the nose is an indication of a lack of attention to detail. Instead of having your mind on work you are thinking about other people or places.

- If the ear is whiter or paler than the rest of the face it is a sign of success and fame.

- A red or pink ear which has a glossy appearance is an indication of intelligence. You understand information or complex problems with ease and know how to use that information.

- If dirty or grey patches suddenly appear on the ear it is a sign that you are about to enter an unlucky period. With patience and care it will soon pass.

- A thick, hard ear is a sign of good fortune. Just when you need support, someone or something turns up to help you.

- Different sized ears are a sign that your plans never work out quite as you expected. When everything seems to be running smoothly there is a minor setback or disturbance.

TYPES OF EAR

Gold Ear

The ear is set slightly higher than the eyebrow and the Heaven wheel and the inner line are close together. The ear has a square shape and the pearl feels hard. The lines of the outer wheel and the inner ring are distinct and the ear is paler than the face (Fig 182).

You are intelligent and creative and have a keen interest in the world around you. The gold ear signifies wealth and career success. Because you do become involved in your work and your interests, relationships with your family may suffer. The gold ear does not combine well with a wood-shaped body.

Wood Ear

The Heaven wheel slopes upwards and the inner ring grows beyond the outer wheel. The ear feels thin and has no ear pearl. The top part of the ear is larger than the middle section (Fig 183).

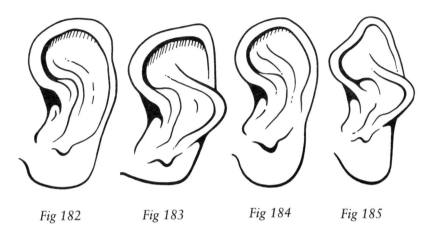

Fig 182   Fig 183   Fig 184   Fig 185

You will take considerable time and effort to establish a career and stable family life. Your patience and effort will be rewarded in the end. This shape is well suited to a wood-shaped body since it denotes a prosperous and happy old age. A less favourable reading is given if the wood ear is combined with a gold or earth-shaped body.

Water Ear

The ears are thick, round and set close to the head and the ear pearl is well rounded. The ears are usually a lighter colour than the facial colouring and are set higher than the eyebrow (Fig 184).

You are quick witted and intelligent. You are not easily upset or flustered and are likely to keep a calm head when others are panicking. Although a good reading is usually given for this ear, it does not always combine well with a fire-shaped person.

Fire Ear

The top of the ear, the Heaven wheel, curves to a point and is slightly higher than the eyebrow. The inner line grows outward over the ear wheel. The ear is long and feels hard to the touch (Fig 185).

You are an independent character and find it hard to accept advice. Your lack of patience and your determination may cause problems within your family or at work although this ear does combine well with a fire-shaped person.

Earth Ear

The ear is fat and large. The ear pearl is full and the outer wheel and the inner ring are well formed and smooth (Fig 186).

The earth ear signifies a prosperous and long life. Your relationships with your family are likely to be strong and affectionate. Their welfare and happiness is as important to you as yours is to them. This ear does not combine well with a wood-shaped body.

Chess Ear

The ear is small, round, thick and hard. The ear is usually lighter in colour than the face and is set slightly higher than the eyebrow (Fig 187).

You enjoy a challenge and have an enterprising nature. Your middle age is likely to be the most prosperous period of your life. If this ear is matched with a gold-shaped body it indicates a stable and happy marriage or long-term relationship. The chess ear does not combine well with a wood-shaped body.

Long Ear (Touching Shoulder Ear)

The ear pearl is long and the ear is fat and thick. The ear is at a higher level than the eyebrow and the skin is clear and glossy (Fig 188).

This ear is an unusual shape and is traditionally regarded as a 'royal ear'. It signifies an authoritative and powerful character. You set yourself ambitious goals and with sustained effort you are likely to achieve them.

Catching Wind Ear

The top and middle of the ear are rounded, large and wide and the ear grows away from the head (Fig 189).

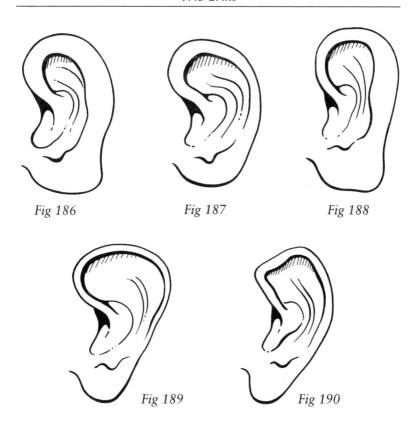

Fig 186   Fig 187   Fig 188

Fig 189   Fig 190

You may have to leave your family or home town at an early age in order to establish your independence or your career. It won't take long for you to achieve your goals or to make a name for yourself. Although you enjoy pursuing your own interests and career you will probably need the support and comfort of a partner to feel fulfilled.

Upper Forward Ear

The ear is S-shaped. The top of the ear slopes forward away from the head but the ear pearl bends backwards so that it is close to the head. The lines of the outer wheel and inner ring are indistinct (Fig 190).

You have an independent nature and prefer to rely on your own resources in order to sort out problems. It takes time for you to relate to others and trust them. It sometimes seems that your life combines a mixture of unexpected lucky incidents and minor accidents or setbacks.

Pig Ear

The pig ear does not have a distinct outer wheel, inner wheel or shape. It feels soft and thick and may grow close to the head or away from the head (Fig 191).

The pig ear is associated with a hot temper. You are easily provoked and although you try to hold your temper your feelings do pour out. Many good opportunities are likely to come your way; some you take but others have passed by the time you have made up your mind. You are fortunte with money but you rarely save or invest it.

Rat Ear

The ear is small and the outer wheel is tightly curled. The top of the ear is full and round and is usually on the same level as the eyebrow (Fig 192).

The rat ear is a sign of an astute and determined nature. You are alert to opportunities for improving your finances, your career or your social life. Your actions are well measured and planned and it is rare for you to act in haste.

Tiger Ear

The ear is thick, hard, small and tightly curled. The lines of the outer wheel and the inner ring are hard to distinguish and are sometimes uneven or broken. The tiger ear is set close to the head (Fig 193).

You have an honest, straightforward nature which is appreciated by your friends and colleagues. You react decisively and impressively; when others are confused, you know when to act and how to act.

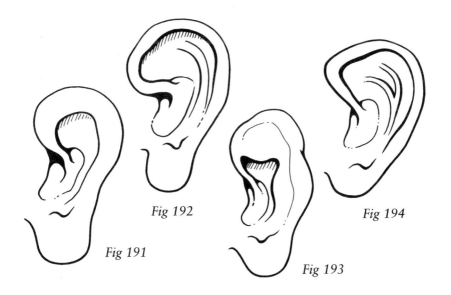

Fig 192

Fig 194

Fig 191

Fig 193

Porcupine Ear

The top of the ear is at a higher level than the eyebrow and the upper part of the ear is wide and full. The ear is hard and straight with a strong appearance (Fig 194).

You are a good judge of people and situations and plan your actions thoughtfully. You are likely to be respected for your vision and your capabilities. There is a streak of wanderlust in your character and you find it hard to put down roots. You also have a relaxed attitude towards finance and are likely to spend your money freely.

BIBLIOGRAPHY

Legge, James (translator), *The Sacred Books of the East*, Vols XVII and XVIII, Oxford University Press, 1855

Legge, James (translator), *Shu Ching (Book of History)*, Vol 3, Chinese Classics, Oxford University Press, 1871

Munro, Donald J., *The Concept of Man in Early China*, Stanford University Press, 1969

Palmer, Kwok, O'Brien, *The Fortune Teller's I Ching*, Rider Century, 1986

Palmer, Martin, *The Elements of Taoism*, Element Books, 1991

About the Editors

Martin Palmer is the director of ICOREC, the International Consultancy on Religion, Education and Culture, based in Manchester. He is a well-known authority on Chinese literature and culture, and author of books on Chinese beliefs and world religions. **Man-Ho Kwok** is a practitioner of Chinese fortune telling, Feng Shui, and face and hand reading. **Joanne O'Brien** is a member of ICOREC and the author of several books on Chinese culture and beliefs.